# The Wiersbe
## BIBLE STUDY SERIES

JUDGES

# The Wiersbe
# BIBLE STUDY SERIES

Accepting the

Challenge to

Confront the

Enemy

David C Cook®
*transforming lives together*

THE WIERSBE BIBLE STUDY SERIES: JUDGES
Published by David C Cook
4050 Lee Vance View
Colorado Springs, CO 80918 U.S.A.

David C Cook Distribution Canada
55 Woodslee Avenue, Paris, Ontario, Canada N3L 3E5

David C Cook U.K., Kingsway Communications
Eastbourne, East Sussex BN23 6NT, England

The graphic circle C logo is a registered trademark of David C Cook.

All excerpts taken from *Be Available*, second edition, published by David C
Cook in 2010 © 1994 Warren W. Wiersbe, ISBN 978-1-4347-0048-3.

LCCN 2014936505
ISBN 978-1-4347-0694-2
eISBN 978-0-7814-1160-8

The Team: Steve Parolini, Karen Lee-Thorp, Amy Konyndyk,
Nick Lee, Tonya Osterhouse, Karen Athen
Cover Design: John Hamilton Design
Cover Photo: iStockphoto

Printed in the United States of America
First Edition 2014

1 2 3 4 5 6 7 8 9 10

042714

# Contents

**Introduction to Judges** . . . . . . . . . . . . . . . . . . . . . . . . . . . . . . 7

**How to Use This Study** . . . . . . . . . . . . . . . . . . . . . . . . . . . . . . 9

**Lesson 1**
The Worst of Times (Judges 1—2) . . . . . . . . . . . . . . . . . . 13

**Lesson 2**
Warfare (Judges 3—5) . . . . . . . . . . . . . . . . . . . . . . . . . . . . .31

**Lesson 3**
Manasseh (Judges 6) . . . . . . . . . . . . . . . . . . . . . . . . . . . . . .51

**Lesson 4**
Victories (Judges 7—8) . . . . . . . . . . . . . . . . . . . . . . . . . . . 69

**Lesson 5**
Kingdom Come (Judges 9—12) . . . . . . . . . . . . . . . . . . . . 87

**Lesson 6**
Two Lights (Judges 13—16) . . . . . . . . . . . . . . . . . . . . . .105

**Lesson 7**
The Center (Judges 17—18) . . . . . . . . . . . . . . . . . . . . . . 123

**Lesson 8**
War and Peace (Judges 19—21) . . . . . . . . . . . . . . . . . . .139

**Bonus Lesson**
Summary and Review . . . . . . . . . . . . . . . . . . . . . . . . . . . .153

# Introduction to Judges

## History Repeats Itself

"Straight ahead lies yesterday!" Dr. Harry Rimmer used to make that statement when referring to biblical history and prophecy; and then he would add, "Future events cast their own shadows before them."

In other words, it's all happened before; and philosopher George Santayana was right: "Those who cannot remember the past are condemned to repeat it." I think we today are living in a period similar to that described in the book of Judges:

- There is no king in Israel.
- People are doing what is right in their own eyes.
- God's people can't seem to work together.
- People are in bondage to various enemies.

## God Rules

The book of Judges makes it clear that God can work in and through all nations, Gentiles as well as Jews. God has "marked out their appointed times in history and the boundaries of their lands" (Acts 17:26). He's the

God of both history and geography. He can use Gentile nations to chasten His own people. He can put one ruler up and bring down another.

While there may not be an obvious *pattern* to history—though historians may search for it—there is definitely a *plan* to history, because God is in control. As Dr. A. T. Pierson used to say, "History is His story." Events that look to us like accidents are really appointments (Rom. 8:28). As dark as the days were in the time of the judges, God was still on the throne, accomplishing His purposes. This ought to encourage us to trust Him and keep serving Him, no matter how grim the prospects might be in this wicked world.

—*Warren W. Wiersbe*

# How to Use This Study

This study is designed for both individual and small-group use. We've divided it into eight lessons—each references one or more chapters in Warren W. Wiersbe's commentary *Be Available* (second edition, David C Cook, 2010). While reading *Be Available* is not a prerequisite for going through this study, the additional insights and background Wiersbe offers can greatly enhance your study experience.

The **Getting Started** questions at the beginning of each lesson offer you an opportunity to record your first thoughts and reactions to the study text. This is an important step in the study process as those "first impressions" often include clues about what it is your heart is longing to discover.

The bulk of the study is found in the **Going Deeper** questions. These dive into the Bible text and, along with helpful excerpts from Wiersbe's commentary, help you examine not only the original context and meaning of the verses but also modern application.

**Looking Inward** narrows the focus down to your personal story. These intimate questions can be a bit uncomfortable at times, but don't shy away from honesty here. This is where you are asked to stand before the mirror of God's Word and look closely at what you see. It's the place to take a good look at yourself in light of the lesson and search for ways in which you can grow in faith.

**Going Forward** is the place where you can commit to paper those things you want or need to do in order to better live out the discoveries you made in the Looking Inward section. Don't skip or skim through this. Take the time to really consider what practical steps you might take to move closer to Christ. Then share your thoughts with a trusted friend who can act as an encourager and accountability partner.

Finally, there is a brief **Seeking Help** section to close the lesson. This is a reminder for you to invite God into your spiritual-growth process. If you choose to write out a prayer in this section, come back to it as you work through the lesson and continue to seek the Holy Spirit's guidance as you discover God's will for your life.

## Tips for Small Groups

A small group is a dynamic thing. One week it might seem like a group of close-knit friends. The next it might seem more like a group of uncomfortable strangers. A small-group leader's role is to read these subtle changes and adjust the tone of the discussion accordingly.

Small groups need to be safe places for people to talk openly. It is through shared wrestling with difficult life issues that some of the greatest personal growth is discovered. But in order for the group to feel safe, participants need to know it's okay *not* to share sometimes. Always invite honest disclosure, but never force someone to speak if he or she isn't comfortable doing so. (A savvy leader will follow up later with a group member who isn't comfortable sharing in a group setting to see if a one-on-one discussion is more appropriate.)

Have volunteers take turns reading excerpts from Scripture or from the commentary. The more each person is involved even in the mundane tasks, the more they'll feel comfortable opening up in more meaningful ways.

The leader should watch the clock and keep the discussion moving. Sometimes there may be more Going Deeper questions than your group can cover in your available time. If you've had a fruitful discussion, it's okay to move on without finishing everything. And if you think the group is getting bogged down on a question or has taken off on a tangent, you can simply say, "Let's go on to question 5." Be sure to save at least ten to fifteen minutes for the Going Forward questions.

Finally, soak your group meetings in prayer—before you begin, during as needed, and always at the end of your time together.

# The Worst of Times

### (JUDGES 1—2)

*Before you begin …*

- *Pray for the Holy Spirit to reveal truth and wisdom as you go through this lesson.*
- *Read Judges 1—2. This lesson references chapter 1, "It Was the Worst of Times," in* Be Available. *It will be helpful for you to have your Bible and a copy of the commentary available as you work through this lesson.*

## Getting Started

*From the Commentary*

FAMILY FEUD LEAVES 69 BROTHERS DEAD!

POWERFUL GOVERNMENT LEADER CAUGHT IN "LOVE NEST."

GANG RAPE LEADS TO VICTIM'S DEATH AND DISMEMBERMENT.

GIRLS AT PARTY KIDNAPPED AND FORCED TO MARRY STRANGERS.

WOMAN JUDGE SAYS TRAVELERS NO LONGER SAFE ON HIGHWAYS.

Sensational headlines like these are usually found on the front page of supermarket tabloids, but the above headlines actually describe some of the events narrated in the book of Judges. What a contrast they are to the closing chapters of the book of Joshua, where you see a nation resting from war and enjoying the riches God had given them in the Promised Land. But the book of Judges pictures Israel suffering from invasion, slavery, poverty, and civil war.

*—Be Available*, page 17

1. According to Judges 1—2, what happened to the nation of Israel after the people were granted the Promised Land? What led to the nation's decay? In what sense was this not just a onetime event, but a pattern in biblical history?

*More to Consider: Instead of exhibiting spiritual fervor, Israel sank into apathy; instead of obeying the Lord, the people moved into apostasy; and instead of the nation enjoying law and order, the land was filled with anarchy. Read Judges 21:25. What does this verse reveal about the reason for Israel's decline? (See also 17:6; 18:1; 19:1.) What are similar examples of a nation's decline in the history of the world? What does this suggest about the role of faith in any nation's success?*

2. Choose one verse or phrase from Judges 1—2 that stands out to you. This could be something you're intrigued by, something that makes you uncomfortable, something that puzzles you, something that resonates with you, or just something you want to examine further. Write that here.

## Going Deeper

*From the Commentary*

Deuteronomy 6 outlined the nation's basic responsibilities: Love and obey Jehovah as the only true God (vv. 1–5); teach your children God's laws (vv. 6–9); be thankful for God's blessings (vv. 10–15); and separate yourself from the worship of the pagan gods in the land of Canaan

(vv. 16–25). Unfortunately, the new generation failed in each of those responsibilities. The people didn't want to "seek ye first the kingdom of God, and his righteousness" (Matt. 6:33); they would rather experiment with the idolatry of the godless nations around them. As a result, Israel plunged into moral, spiritual, and political disaster.

—*Be Available*, page 18

3. One of two things was true in this story: either the older generation had failed to instruct their children and grandchildren in the ways of the Lord, or, if they had faithfully taught them, then the new generation had refused to submit to God's law and follow God's ways. Which do you think it was? Why? Describe the various stages of Israel's decline and fall.

## From the Commentary

The book of Judges begins with a series of victories and defeats that took place after the death of Joshua. The boundary lines for the twelve tribes had been determined years before (Josh. 13—22), but the people had not yet fully claimed their inheritance by defeating and dislodging the entrenched inhabitants of the land. When Joshua was an old man, the Lord said to him, "You are old, advanced in years, and there remains very much land yet to be possessed" (Josh. 13:1 NKJV). The people of Israel *owned* all the land, but they didn't *possess* all of it, and therefore they couldn't *enjoy* all of it.

Initially the people of Israel wisely sought God's guidance and asked the Lord which tribe was to engage the enemy first. Perhaps God told Judah to go first because Judah was the kingly tribe (Gen. 49:8–9). Judah believed God's promise, obeyed God's counsel, and even asked the people of the tribe of Simeon to go to battle with them. Since Leah had given birth to Judah and Simeon, these tribes were blood brothers (Gen. 35:23). Incidentally, Simeon actually had its inheritance within the tribe of Judah (Josh. 19:1).

When Joshua was Israel's leader, all the tribes worked together in obeying the will of God. In the book of Judges, however, you don't find the nation working together as a unit. When God needed someone to deliver His people, He called that person out of one of the tribes and told him or her what to do. In obedience to the Lord, Moses had appointed Joshua as his successor, but later God didn't command Joshua to name a successor.

*—Be Available*, page 19

4. Why do you think God didn't command Joshua to name a successor? How are the circumstances described in this section of Judges similar to what's happening in the church today?

## From Today's World

In the time of the judges, war was not only common but pretty much expected as the various tribes and peoples vied for power and position in the land. Today, the very same issues drive neighboring nations—and even neighboring towns—to fight for something they believe in, whatever the cost. (And the cost can often be great.) Today's church is put in a precarious position because of such world events, which threaten to divide its members over controversial issues. Few issues are more divisive than that of war and the role of the military in promoting peace around the globe. While many believe that greater military strength translates into a more assured peace, others argue that peace ought to come without the threat of war as its foundation.

5. What lessons (if any) can we take from the time of the judges regarding a proper and right response to war? What role did God play in the time of the judges? How did the people respond to God's direction? How has God's role changed in times of war and conflict today? How does Jesus'

narrative in the New Testament reveal new truths about how God invites His people to respond to war?

## From the Commentary

Jerusalem (Judg. 1:8) was Israel's next trophy, but though the Israelites conquered the city, they didn't occupy it (v. 21). That wasn't done until the time of David (2 Sam. 5:7). Judah and Benjamin were neighboring tribes, and since the city was located on their border, both tribes were involved in attacking it. Later, Jerusalem would become "the city of David" and the capital of Israel.

They next attacked the area south and west of Jerusalem, which included Hebron (Judg. 1:9–10, 20). This meant fighting in the hill country, the south (Negev), and the foothills. Joshua had promised Hebron to Caleb because of his faithfulness to the Lord at Kadesh Barnea (Num. 13—14; Josh. 14:6–15; Deut. 1:34–36). Sheshai, Ahiman, and Talmai were descendants of the giant Anak, whose people had frightened ten of the twelve Jewish spies who first explored the land (Num. 13:22, 28). Even though Caleb and Joshua, the other two spies, had the

faith needed to overcome the enemy, the people wouldn't
listen to them.

—*Be Available*, pages 20–21

6. Caleb and Joshua stayed true to God, even when the majority of the
Israelites disagreed with them about trying to conquer the Promised Land
(Num. 13:26–33). What was Caleb's reward (Judg. 1:1–11)? Why was
Caleb's reward so appropriate considering his role in the earlier review of
Canaan? What are some ways God rewards faithfulness today?

## From the Commentary

In Judges 1:22–26, the tribe of Ephraim joined with
the western section of the tribe of Manasseh and, with
the Lord's help, they took the city of Bethel. This city
was important to the Jews because of its connection
with the patriarchs (Gen. 12:8; 13:3; 28:10–12; 35:1–7).
Apparently it hadn't been taken during the conquest
under Joshua, or if it had been, the Jews must have lost
control.

—*Be Available*, pages 21–22

7. How was the saving of the informer's family (Judg. 1:22–26) similar to what happened to Rahab when Jericho was destroyed (Josh. 2; 6)? Why did the rescued man and his family refuse to stay with the Israelites, with whom they could be safe while learning about the true and living God? How is this similar to the way people sometimes respond to God's offer of salvation even today?

*From the Commentary*

Benjamin, Ephraim, Manasseh, Zebulun, Asher, Naphtali, and Dan all failed to overcome the enemy and had to allow these godless nations to continue living in their tribal territories. The enemy even chased the tribe of Dan out of the plains into the mountains! The Jebusites remained in Jerusalem (Judg. 1:21), and the Canaanites who remained were finally pressed "into forced labor" when the Jews became stronger (v. 28 NIV). Eventually Solomon conscripted these Canaanite peoples to build the temple (1 Kings 9:20–22; 2 Chron. 8:7–8), but this was no compensation for the problems the Canaanites caused the Jews. This series of tribal defeats was the first indication that Israel was no longer walking by faith and trusting God to give them victory.

The priests possessed a copy of the book of Deuteronomy and were commanded to read it publicly to the nation every sabbatical year during the Feast of Tabernacles (Deut. 31:9–13). Had they been faithful to do their job, the spiritual leaders would have read Deuteronomy 7 and warned the Israelites not to spare their pagan neighbors. The priests also would have reminded the people of God's promises that He would help them defeat their enemies (Deut. 31:1–8). It was by receiving and obeying the book of the law that Joshua had grown in faith and courage (Josh. 1:1–9; Rom. 10:17), and that same Word would have enabled the new generation to overcome their enemies and claim their inheritance.

—*Be Available*, pages 22–23

8. The first step the new generation took toward defeat and slavery was to neglect God's Word (Judg. 2:1–3). What might motivate a people to do that? How is that still happening in today's church?

*More to Consider: Was it cruel and unjust for God to command Israel to exterminate the nations in Canaan? Consider the passages of Genesis 15:16 and 2 Peter 3:9. In what ways was their society, and especially their religion, unspeakably wicked? How did this justify God's response? (See also Rom. 1:18–32.)*

## From the Commentary

In this day of "pluralism," when society contains people of opposing beliefs and lifestyles, it's easy to get confused and start thinking that *tolerance* is the same as *approval*. It isn't. In a democracy, the law gives people the freedom to worship as they please, and I must exercise patience and tolerance with those who believe and practice things that I feel God has condemned in His Word. The church today doesn't wield the sword (Rom. 13) and therefore it has no authority to eliminate people who disagree with the Christian faith. But we do have the obligation before God to maintain a separate walk so we won't become defiled by those who disagree with us (2 Cor. 6:14—7:1). We must seek by prayer, witness, and loving persuasion to win those to Christ who as yet haven't trusted Him.

—*Be Available*, page 24

9. What happened when the Jews became accustomed to the sinful ways of their pagan neighbors (Judg. 2:10–13)? Why did they become interested in the way they worshipped? How is this like today's believers becoming "friends with the world"?

## From the Commentary

The sin in our lives that we fail to conquer will eventually conquer us. The people of Israel found themselves enslaved to one pagan nation after another as the Lord kept His word and chastened His people. Consider the sins of that new generation.

**They forgot what the Lord had done (Judg. 2:6–10).** At that point in Israel's history, Joshua stood next to Moses as a great hero, and yet the new generation didn't recognize who he was or what he had done. In his popular novel *1984*, George Orwell wrote, "Who controls the past controls the future: who controls the present controls the past." Once they got in control of the present, both Hitler and Stalin rewrote past history so they could control future events, and for a time it worked. How important it is for each new generation to recognize and appreciate the great men and women who helped to build and protect their nation! It's disturbing when "revisionist" historians debunk the heroes and heroines of the past and almost make them criminals.

**They forsook what the Lord had said (Judg. 2:11–13).** Had they remembered Joshua, they would have known his "farewell speeches" given to the leaders and the people of Israel (Josh. 23—24). Had they known those speeches, they would have known the law of Moses, for in his final messages, Joshua emphasized the covenant God had made with Israel and the responsibility Israel had to keep it. When you forget the Word of God, you are in danger of forsaking the God of the Word, which explains why Israel turned to the vile and vicious worship of Baal.

**They forfeited what the Lord had promised (Judg. 2:14–15).** When they went out to fight their enemies, Israel was defeated, because the Lord wasn't with His people. This is what Moses had said would happen (Deut. 28:25–26), but that isn't all: *Israel's enemies eventually became their masters!* God permitted one nation after another to invade the Promised Land and enslave His people, making life so miserable for them that they cried out for help. Had the Jews obeyed the Lord, their armies would have been victorious, but left to themselves they were defeated and humiliated.

**They failed to learn from what the Lord did (Judg. 2:16–23).** Whenever Israel turned away from the Lord to worship idols, He chastened them severely, and when in their misery they turned back to Him, He liberated them. But just as soon as they were free and their situation was comfortable again, Israel went right back into the same old sins.

—*Be Available*, pages 26–27

10. Review Judges 2:6–23. How did each of these sins lead to the nation's downfall? What are modern equivalents of these sins that today's church must overcome? What are some ways we can learn from what the Lord did in history to help us make better choices in how we live out our faith in a fallen world?

## Looking Inward

Take a moment to reflect on all that you've explored thus far in this study of Judges 1—2. Review your notes and answers and think about how each of these things matters in your life today.

*Tips for Small Groups: To get the most out of this section, form pairs or trios and have group members take turns answering these questions. Be honest and as open as you can in this discussion, but most of all, be encouraging and supportive of others. Be sensitive to those who are going through particularly difficult times and don't press for people to speak if they're uncomfortable doing so.*

11. Think about a time when you rebelled against God. What led to that rebellion? What did you do in your rebellion? What brought you back to God?

12. What are some ways your loyalty to God has been tested? Why do people or circumstances test your faith? What happens to faith when it's tested? What happens when you fail those tests? When you pass them? How is God glorified either way?

13. What are some ways you've chosen to directly ignore what you know to be God's word? Why would you choose to defy what you know is true? How is your relationship with God compromised when you pick and choose what to obey in Scripture? How is this different from being wise in interpreting Scripture?

## Going Forward

14. Think of one or two things that you have learned that you'd like to work on in the coming week. Remember that this is all about quality, not quantity. It's better to work on one specific area of life and do it well than to work on many and do poorly (or to be so overwhelmed that you simply don't try).

Do you want to seek the strength to hold on to God's promises when things look bleak? Be specific. Go back through Judges 1—2 and put a star next to the phrase or verse that is most encouraging to you. Consider memorizing this verse.

> *Real-Life Application Ideas: The nation of Israel was notorious for "forgetting" what God had already done for them and making the same mistakes over and over again in following the ways of a wicked world instead of a holy God. Think back on your own spiritual history. What are some of the great things God has done for you that could inspire you to keep moving toward God, even when the world tempts you in a different direction? Make a list of these things and keep them in your wallet or purse to remind you of how God has loved you and shaped you in the past, and how He promises to do so in the future.*

## Seeking Help

15. Write a prayer below (or simply pray one in silence), inviting God to work on your mind and heart in those areas you've noted in the Going Forward section. Be honest about your desires and fears.

*Notes for Small Groups:*

- *Look for ways to put into practice the things you wrote in the Going Forward section. Talk with other group members about your ideas and commit to being accountable to one another.*

- *During the coming week, ask the Holy Spirit to continue to reveal truth to you from what you've read and studied.*

- *Before you start the next lesson, read Judges 3—5. For more in-depth lesson preparation, read chapters 2 and 3, "The Weapons of Our Warfare" and "'Two Are Better Than One, and Three Are Better Still,'" in* Be Available.

# Warfare
## (JUDGES 3—5)

*Before you begin …*
- *Pray for the Holy Spirit to reveal truth and wisdom as you go through this lesson.*
- *Read Judges 3—5. This lesson references chapters 2 and 3 in* Be Available. *It will be helpful for you to have your Bible and a copy of the commentary available as you work through this lesson.*

## Getting Started

*From the Commentary*

"The weapons we fight with are not the weapons of the world." That statement could have been made by a space alien in a sci-fi novel, but it wasn't. The apostle Paul wrote those words to the believers in Corinth (2 Cor. 10:4 NIV), reminding them of a principle every Christian needs to take to heart: *When God goes to war, He usually chooses the most unlikely soldiers, hands them the most unusual weapons, and accomplishes through them the most unpredictable results.*

For example, God gave Shamgar an ox goad, and with it he killed 600 men (Judg. 3:31). Jael used a hammer and tent peg to kill a captain (4:21), and Gideon routed the whole Midianite army with only pitchers and torches as weapons (7:20). Samson slaughtered 1,000 Philistines using the jawbone of an ass (15:15), and young David killed the giant Goliath with a stone hurled from a shepherd's sling (1 Sam. 17). West Point isn't likely to offer courses on how to use these weapons.

—*Be Available*, page 31

1. Though our world has changed dramatically since the days of the judges, the "world system" is the same because human nature hasn't changed (1 John 2:15–17). What does this suggest about the persistence of spiritual battles? (See Eph. 6:10–19.) What are some of the characteristics of believers who are prepared for these battles? What are the essentials for victory?

2. Choose one verse or phrase from Judges 3—5 that stands out to you. This could be something you're intrigued by, something that makes you

uncomfortable, something that puzzles you, something that resonates with you, or just something you want to examine further. Write that here.

## Going Deeper

*From the Commentary*

> In Judges 3, you will find "five lords of the Philistines" (v. 3) and the king of Moab called "lord" (v. 25); but more importantly "the Lord," meaning Jehovah God, is named fifteen times in these thirty-one verses. That lets us know who is really in charge. The Presbyterian missionary leader A. T. Pierson used to say that "history is His story," and he was right. As He executes His divine decrees, God never violates human responsibility, but He does rule and overrule in the affairs of individuals and nations to accomplish His great purposes on this earth.
>
> The early church prayed, "Lord, You *are* God!" and they gladly confessed that their enemies could do only "whatever Your hand and Your purpose determined before to be done" (Acts 4:24, 28 NKJV). Poet T. S. Eliot said, "Destiny waits in the hand of God, not in the hands of statesmen."

The tribe of Judah was not able to hold on to the key Philistine cities they had taken (1:18; 3:3), and as we saw in chapter 1, the other tribes failed to conquer the Canaanite nations. These surviving nations adopted a "good neighbor" policy toward Israel that eventually defeated Israel from within. Sometimes Satan comes as a lion to devour, but often he comes as a serpent to deceive (1 Peter 5:8; 2 Cor. 11:3).

—*Be Available*, page 32

3. How does the quote by Eliot relate to the experience of Judah and the other tribes? How does it apply to the modern church? Why did God choose not to judge Israel for sparing the Canaanite nations in this story (Judg. 3:1–4), even though history has shown that He judged them on other occasions for the same error?

*More to Consider: How did God respond to the Israelites when they obeyed Him? (See Gen. 23:6; 26:26–33; 30:27; 39:5.) How did this provide them with an opportunity to share God's truth with others? (See Deut. 4:1–13.) What does this tell us about the broader impact of disobeying God?*

## From the Commentary

The name of the king of Mesopotamia means "doubly wicked Cushan," which may have been a nickname that his enemies gave him. We aren't told where he invaded Israel, although logically the attack would have come from the north; nor are we told how much of the land he subjugated for those eight painful years. Since the deliverer God raised up was from Judah, it's possible that the invading army had penetrated that far south in Israel when the Lord decided to intervene on behalf of His suffering people.

Charles Spurgeon said that God never allows His people to sin successfully. Their sin will either destroy them or it will invite the chastening hand of God. If the history of Israel teaches the contemporary church anything, it's the obvious lesson that "righteousness exalts a nation, but sin is a disgrace to any people" (Prov. 14:34 NIV).

There's no evidence that the people repented of their sins when they cried out to God for help, but the Lord responded to their plight and gave them a deliverer.

—*Be Available*, page 35

4. How was God's response to the people's plight (Judg. 3:7–11) similar to the exodus experience? In what way did God not allow His people to "sin successfully" in this story? What was the lesson God intended to teach the people through all this?

## From the Commentary

Unlike Moses, who appointed Joshua to lead Israel, the judges didn't have the authority to name a successor. When God called men and women to serve as judges, they obeyed, did His work, and then passed from the scene. One would hope that their godly influence would make a lasting difference in the spiritual life of the nation, but such wasn't the case. No sooner was a judge off the scene than the people were back to worshipping Baal and forsaking the Lord.

You would think that gratitude alone would have motivated the people of Israel to obey the Lord and be faithful to His covenant, especially after enduring eighteen years of painful servitude. And think of all that God had done for Israel in the past! They would have been a forgotten little nation if God hadn't loved them and chosen them for Himself (Deut. 7:1–11). They would have perished in Egypt or in the wilderness if God hadn't delivered them and cared for them. They would have died on the battlefields of Canaan if the Lord hadn't given them victory over their enemies. They would have been wallowing in moral sewage if the Lord hadn't given them His law and the priests to teach it to them.

—*Be Available*, page 37

5. Why wasn't God's presence in the tabernacle or His promises in the covenant enough for the Israelites? What more did they want? Where did they get this idea? What are some things that many Christians want today that draw them to embrace the ways of the modern world?

## From the Commentary

Only one verse is devoted to Shamgar, and it isn't even stated that he was a judge. Judges 5:6–7 indicates that he was a contemporary with Deborah and Barak. "Son of Anath" may mean that he was from the town of Beth Anath in Naphtali (1:33), which was also the tribe Barak came from (4:6; see 5:18). Since Anath was the name of a Canaanite goddess of war, perhaps "son of Anath" was a nickname that meant "son of battle"—that is, a mighty warrior.

What was significant about Shamgar was the weapon that he used. An ox goad was a strong pole about eight feet long. At one end was a sharp metal point for prodding the oxen and at the other end a spade for cleaning the dirt off the plow. It was the closest thing Shamgar could find to a spear because the enemy had confiscated the weapons of the Israelites (5:8; see 1 Sam. 13:19–22).

Here was a man who obeyed God and defeated the enemy even though his resources were limited. Instead of complaining about not possessing a sword or spear, Shamgar gave what he had to the Lord, and the Lord used it. Joseph Parker said, "What is a feeble instrument in the hands of one man is a mighty instrument in the hands of another, simply because the spirit of that other burns with holy determination to accomplish the work that has to be done."

Shamgar may have killed all 600 Philistines at one time in one place (2 Sam. 8:8–12), but it's also possible that 600 is a cumulative total. An ox goad would be an unwieldy weapon to use if 600 soldiers had attacked Shamgar at one time. Since we don't know the details, we must not speculate. It's just encouraging to know that God enabled him to overcome the enemy though his resources were limited.

—*Be Available*, pages 40–41

6. What impression does Judges 3:31 give about Shamgar? What does his legacy as a judge teach us about working with limited resources? How can this inspire church workers today?

## From the Commentary

The cast of characters in the drama of Judges 4 is as follows:

**Jabin:** King of Hazor in Canaan; a tyrant

**Deborah:** a Jewish judge; a woman of faith and courage

**Barak:** a reluctant Jewish general

**Sisera:** captain of Jabin's army

**Heber:** a Kenite neighbor, at peace with Jabin

**Jael:** wife of Heber; handy with a hammer

**Jehovah God:** in charge of wars and weather

Now let the drama unfold.

Jabin is the key person in act one (4:1–3), for God raised him up to discipline the people of Israel. For eighty years, the Jews had enjoyed rest because of the leadership of Ehud, the longest period of peace recorded in the book of Judges. But no sooner was this godly judge removed than the people lapsed back into idolatry, and God had to punish them (Judg. 2:10–19).

—*Be Available*, page 45

7. Was the Israelites' season of rest (3:30) an example of true spiritual revival? Why or why not? (See 4:1–3.) What are the key differences between simple reform and true revival?

## From the Commentary

In act two (4:4–7), God had raised up a courageous woman named Deborah (which means "bee") to be the judge in the land. This was an act of grace, but it was also an act of humiliation for the Jews, for they lived in a male-dominated society that wanted only mature male leadership. "As for my people, children are their oppressors, and women rule over them" (Isa. 3:12). For God to give His people a woman judge was to treat them like little children, which is exactly what they were when it came to spiritual things.

Deborah was both a judge and a prophetess. Moses' sister Miriam was a prophetess (Ex. 15:20), and later biblical history introduces us to Huldah (2 Kings 22:14), Noadiah (Neh. 6:14), Anna (Luke 2:36), and the four daughters of Philip (Acts 21:9). God called Deborah a prophetess and a judge, but she saw herself as a *mother* to her people. "I Deborah arose, that I arose a mother in Israel" (Judg. 5:7). The wayward Jews were her children, and she welcomed them and counseled them.

—*Be Available*, pages 46–47

8. Why was it so controversial to have a judge who was a woman? What was the benefit of being both a judge and a prophetess? What are some ways churches today continue to struggle with the role of women in the church? How can Deborah's story help us respond with wisdom to this question?

*More to Consider: In act three, we aren't told that Barak was a judge, which explains why he got his orders from Deborah, God's appointed leader in the land. Barak was from Naphtali, one of the tribes that would send volunteers to the battlefield (Judg. 4:6). Like Moses before him (Ex. 3—4), and Gideon (Judg. 6) and Jeremiah (Jer. 1) after him, Barak hesitated when told what God wanted him to do.*

*We know that "God's commandments are God's enablements" and that we should obey His will in spite of circumstances, feelings, or consequences. But we don't always do it! Was Barak's response a sign of unbelief or a mark of humility? Explain.*

*Barak enlisted 10,000 men from his own tribe of Naphtali and the neighboring tribe of Zebulun (Judg. 4:6, 10; 5:14, 18). Later, volunteers from the tribes of Benjamin, Ephraim, and Machir (v. 14), and Issachar (v. 15), joined these men, and the army grew to 40,000 men (v. 8). It's possible that the original 10,000 soldiers initiated the campaign that lured Sisera into the trap, and then the other 30,000 joined them for the actual battle and "mopping up" operation. The tribes that were summoned but refused to come were Reuben, Dan, Asher, and Gilead (vv. 15–17).*

*How was what Deborah and Barak did an act of faith? In what ways were they counting on God?*

## From the Commentary

The Lord is the leading actor in the fourth act (4:11–23). He not only controlled the enemy army and brought it into the trap, but He also controlled the weather and used a storm to defeat Sisera's troops.

The Canaanites depended on their 900 iron chariots to give them the advantage they needed as they met the Jewish army (1:19; see Josh. 17:18). What they didn't know was that the Lord would send a fierce rainstorm that would make the Kishon River overflow and turn the battlefield into a sea of mud (Judg. 5:20–22). The water and mud would severely impede the mobility of the Canaanite chariots and horses, and this situation would make it easy for the Israelite soldiers to attack and slaughter the enemy. The trap worked, and the enemy army was wiped out.

Along with the storm from the heavens and the flood from the swollen river, God sent confusion in the minds of the enemy troops. The word translated "routed" (4:15 NKJV) means "confused, thrown into panic." This is what God had done to Pharaoh's charioteers in the Red Sea (Ex. 14:24) and would later do to the Philistines in Samuel's day (1 Sam. 7:10).

One thing that helped to confuse and frighten the Canaanites was the sudden appearance of torrential rain during the traditional dry season. Since Sisera wouldn't have taken his chariots to the fields if he had suspected any kind of bad weather, we can safely assume that this battle was fought during the June-to-September dry season. When you remember that the Canaanite god Baal was the god of storms, you can see how the sudden change of weather could have affected the superstitious Canaanites. Had their own god Baal turned against them? Was the God of Israel stronger than Baal? If so, then the battle was already lost, and the wisest thing the soldiers could do was flee.

—*Be Available*, pages 48–50

9. What does the sudden appearance of torrential rain during the dry season tell us about God's creativity in accomplishing His plans? What did the storms reveal about the God of Israel as compared to the Canaanite god Baal? How should that comparison have affected the Israelites for the rest of their lives?

## From the Commentary

When they wanted to celebrate special occasions, the Jewish people often expressed themselves in song, so the writer shifts from narrative prose to jubilant poetry in the final act of this drama (5:1–31). Future generations might forget what the history book said, but they were not likely to forget a festive song. (For other examples, see Ex. 15, Deut. 32, 2 Sam. 1:17–27, and Ps. 18.) The personal pronouns in Judges 5:7, 9, and 13 indicate that this was Deborah's victory song, but just as Barak joined her in the battle, so he joined her in the victory celebration.

A poem or song isn't something you can easily outline because it's a spontaneous emotional expression that often defies analysis. Unlike classical English poetry, Hebrew poetry contains recurring themes, expressed in different ways and frequent outbursts of praise and prayer. The following outline is only a suggested approach to this magnificent song of victory.

In verses 1–9, Deborah and Barak praise the Lord for all that He did for His people. He gave unity to the leaders so that Barak could assemble an army (v. 2; and see v. 9). The same God who gave Israel victory in the past would give them victory again (vv. 4–5). Israel had entered into a covenant with the Lord at Mount Sinai, and He would fulfill His promises to His special people.

—*Be Available*, page 52

10. What themes are repeated in the song in Judges 5? How are they still relevant today? How does the closing prayer (v. 31) contrast the Lord's enemies with the people who love God? In what ways was the battle at Megiddo more than just a conflict between opposing armies?

# Looking Inward

Take a moment to reflect on all that you've explored thus far in this study of Judges 3—5. Review your notes and answers and think about how each of these things matters in your life today.

*Tips for Small Groups: To get the most out of this section, form pairs or trios and have group members take turns answering these questions. Be honest and as open as you can in this discussion, but most of all, be encouraging and supportive of others. Be sensitive to those who are going through particularly difficult times and don't press for people to speak if they're uncomfortable doing so.*

11. What are some of the "weapons" you keep at the ready to face spiritual battles? How do you use those weapons? How do you keep them sharp? What happens when you don't care for those weapons?

12. God used storms to help the Israelites defeat the Canaanites. Have you ever experienced God's intervention in the natural world? If so, explain. How did you know it was God directing the circumstances?

13. The final piece of this little drama is a celebration of God's goodness and faithfulness. What are some ways you praise God for the victories in your life (whether small or large)? Why is it important to praise God in those moments?

## Going Forward

14. Think of one or two things that you have learned that you'd like to work on in the coming week. Remember that this is all about quality, not quantity. It's better to work on one specific area of life and do it well than to work on many and do poorly (or to be so overwhelmed that you simply don't try).

Do you want to work on being spiritually prepared for challenges to your faith? Be specific. Go back through Judges 3—5 and put a star next to the phrase or verse that is most encouraging to you. Consider memorizing this verse.

*Real-Life Application Ideas: Judges is packed with stories of war, of God's hand in delivering the Israelites, or in teaching them some truth through the course of their defeat. This week, think about the various battles you're engaged in. Perhaps you're in a battle at work or with a family member. Maybe you're experiencing difficulty with a neighbor. As you consider the various battles you're in, ask God for wisdom in dealing with them. Are there lessons to be learned from the battle itself? From admitting you might be wrong? Allow God (and the wisdom of trusted friends) to lead you to the right response, rather than having to be right.*

## Seeking Help

15. Write a prayer below (or simply pray one in silence), inviting God to work on your mind and heart in those areas you've noted in the Going Forward section. Be honest about your desires and fears.

*Notes for Small Groups:*

- *Look for ways to put into practice the things you wrote in the Going Forward section. Talk with other group members about your ideas and commit to being accountable to one another.*

- *During the coming week, ask the Holy Spirit to continue to reveal truth to you from what you've read and studied.*

- *Before you start the next lesson, read Judges 6. For more in-depth lesson preparation, read chapter 4, "God's Man in Manasseh," in* Be Available.

# Manasseh
## (JUDGES 6)

*Before you begin...*
- *Pray for the Holy Spirit to reveal truth and wisdom as you go through this lesson.*
- *Read Judges 6. This lesson references chapter 4 in* Be Available. *It will be helpful for you to have your Bible and a copy of the commentary available as you work through this lesson.*

## Getting Started

*From the Commentary*

You have a garden, and you work hard all spring and summer to make that garden produce abundantly. But every year, just about the time you're ready to gather in the harvest, your neighbors swoop down and take your produce away from you by force. This goes on year after year, and there's nothing you can do about it.

If you can imagine that scenario, then you'll have some

idea of the suffering the Jews experienced every harvest when the Midianites made their annual raids. For seven years, God allowed the Midianites and their allies to ravage "the land of milk and honey," leaving the people in the deepest poverty.

About the time of the eighth Midianite invasion, God called a farmer in Manasseh named Gideon to become the deliverer of His people.

—*Be Available*, page 59

1. Why would God allow so much devastation in the "land of milk and honey"? What did He intend to teach the people through this season of war? Why did He wait until the eighth invasion to call Gideon as deliverer?

*More to Consider: Gideon started his career as somewhat of a coward (Judg. 6), then became a conqueror (7:1—8:21), and ended his career as a compromiser (8:22–35). More space is dedicated to Gideon in the book of Judges (100 verses) than to any other judge. Why is it significant that Gideon's personal struggles with his faith are recorded here? How can his story inspire struggling believers even today?*

2. Choose one verse or phrase from Judges 6 that stands out to you. This could be something you're intrigued by, something that makes you uncomfortable, something that puzzles you, something that resonates with you, or just something you want to examine further. Write that here.

## Going Deeper

*From the Commentary*

"The LORD has forsaken us!" was Gideon's response to the Lord's message (Judg. 6:13 NKJV); and yet the Lord had given Israel proof of His personal concern.

"My son, do not despise the chastening of the LORD, nor detest His correction; for whom the LORD loves He corrects, just as a father the son in whom he delights" (Prov. 3:11–12 NKJV; and see Heb. 12:5–11). Charles Spurgeon said, "The Lord does not permit His children to sin successfully." God is not a "permissive parent" who allows His children to do as they please, for His ultimate purpose is that they might be "conformed to the image of His Son" (Rom. 8:29). The Father wants to be able to look at each member of His spiritual family and say, "This is

My beloved child, in whom I am well pleased" (see Matt. 3:17; 12:18; 17:5).

—*Be Available*, page 60

3. In what ways is chastening evidence of God's hatred for sin and His love for His people? How does chastening show that God wants His very best for His children? Why does God choose to directly confront His people on some occasions, while letting them fumble around without intervention on others? What does this reveal about the way God works?

## From the Commentary

The Midianites organized a coalition of nations to invade the land (Judg. 6:3), and all that Israel could do was flee to the hills and hide from the enemy. When the Jews returned to their homes, they found only devastation, and they had to face another year without adequate food.

Previous to this, an angel of the Lord, probably the Son of God, had come to Bochim to reprove Israel for her sins (2:1–5), and now an unnamed prophet came to repeat the message. Often in the Old Testament, when the

Lord denounced His people for their disobedience, He reminded them of the wonderful way He had delivered them from Egypt. He also reminded them of His generosity in giving them the land and helping them overcome their enemies. If the Jews were suffering from Gentile bondage, it wasn't God's fault! He had given them everything they needed.

—*Be Available*, page 61

4. Why did God remind the people about how He had helped them before? Why didn't the people remember this without God's reminder? How was this approach similar to the way the apostles admonished the believers? (See Eph. 4:1 and Col. 3:1–4.)

## From Today's World

In a world where "tolerance" has become the battle cry of many, it's often difficult to know when someone needs "chastening." A society that champions all beliefs and all lifestyles in an effort to accept everyone leaves little room for criticism and questioning of behavior. This mind-set has been creeping into the church, too, often claiming Jesus as its source. But there's a difference between accepting all people as directed by the teachings of Christ and approving of all people's behavior and choices.

5. How does the trend toward "tolerance" negatively affect the church's ability to find and maintain its identity? What is the difference between tolerating beliefs and accepting all people as children of God? How can today's church become a welcoming place for all people while still celebrating and teaching what it means to follow Christ?

*From the Commentary*

> The people were crying out to the Lord for help (Judg. 6:7), as people usually do when they're in trouble. The Israelites gave no evidence of real repentance, but their affliction moved God's loving heart. "In all their affliction he was afflicted" (Isa. 63:9). "He does not treat us as our sins deserve or repay us according to our iniquities" (Ps. 103:10 NIV). God in His mercy doesn't give us what we do deserve, and in His grace, He gives us what we don't deserve.
>
> When you consider the kind of man Gideon was at this time, you wonder why God selected him, but God often

chooses the "weak things of the world" to accomplish
great things for His glory (1 Cor. 1:26–29). Gideon's
family worshipped Baal (Judg. 6:25–32), although we
have no reason to believe that Gideon joined them. When
Gideon called himself "the least in my father's house" (v.
15), he may have been suggesting that his family treated
him like an outcast because he didn't worship Baal.
Gideon wasn't a man of strong faith or courage, and God
had to patiently work with him to prepare him for leadership. God is always ready to make us what we ought to
be if we're willing to submit to His will (Eph. 2:10; Phil.
2:12–13).

—*Be Available*, page 62

6. As the conversation unfolded, what were Gideon's responses to God's
words (Judg. 6:11–24)? What did his responses reveal about his heart?
What would it take to change his perception of God?

*From the Commentary*

Gideon's first response was to question *God's concern* for His people, but then he questioned *God's wisdom* in choosing him to be the nation's deliverer. The Lord's statements recorded in verses 12 and 14 should have given Gideon all the assurance he needed, but he wouldn't believe God's Word. In this he was like Moses (Ex. 3:7–12), whose story Gideon surely knew since he was acquainted with Hebrew history (Judg. 6:13).

It has often been said that "God's commandments are God's enablements." Once God has called and commissioned us, all we have to do is obey Him by faith, and He will do the rest. God cannot lie and God never fails. Faith means obeying God in spite of what we see, how we feel, or what the consequences might be. Our modern "practical" world laughs at faith without realizing that people live by faith all day long. "If there was no faith, there would be no living in this world," wrote humorist Josh Billings nearly a century ago. "We couldn't even eat hash with safety."

Gideon's statement about the poverty of his family is a bit perplexing in light of the fact that he had ten servants who assisted him (v. 27). It may be that the clan of Abiezer, to which Gideon's family belonged, was not an important clan in Manasseh, or perhaps Gideon's statement was simply the standard way to respond to a compliment, as when people used to sign their letters "Your Obedient Servant." In any event, Gideon seemed to think that God could *do* nothing because he and his family *were* nothing.

—*Be Available*, pages 62–63

7. Review Judges 6:14–24. What should Gideon's response have been when God revealed His will to him? Why did he question God? How did God respond to Gideon's argument?

## From the Commentary

Gideon asked for a sign to assure him that it was really the Lord who was speaking to him (1 Cor. 1:22), and the Lord was gracious to accommodate Himself to Gideon's unbelief. Gideon prepared a sacrifice, which was a costly thing to do at a time when food was scarce. An ephah of flour was about a half a bushel, enough to make bread for a family for several days. It probably took him an hour to dress the meat and prepare the unleavened cakes, but God waited for him to return and then consumed the offering by bringing fire from the rock.

The sudden appearance of the fire and disappearance of the visitor convinced Gideon that indeed he had seen God and spoken to Him, and this frightened him even more. Since the Jews believed it was fatal for sinful man to look upon God, Gideon was sure he would die. The human heart is indeed deceitful: Gideon asked to see a sign, and after seeing it, he was sure that the God who gave him the sign would now kill him! There is always "joy and peace in believing" (Rom. 15:13), but unbelief brings fear and worry.

—*Be Available*, page 64

8. How did God's message of peace to Gideon help prepare him for fighting a war? Why is being at peace with God critical when people face daunting challenges? How does peace with God build confidence?

*More to Consider: Before David killed the giant Goliath within sight of two armies, he learned to trust God by killing lions and bears in the field where nobody saw it but God (1 Sam. 17:32–37). How is this true in Gideon's story? What does this teach us about how God prepares us in life? What is God preparing us for (Matt. 25:21)?*

## From the Commentary

Gideon decided to obey the Lord at night when the village was asleep. This showed his fear (Judg. 6:27); he wasn't sure God could or would see him through. "Why are you so fearful? How is it that you have no faith?" (Mark 4:40 NKJV). "Behold, God is my salvation, I will trust and not be afraid" (Isa. 12:2 NKJV). After all the encouragements God had given him, Gideon's faith should have been strong, but before we judge him, we'd better look at ourselves and see how much *we* trust the Lord.

It's worth noting that true believers can't build an altar to the Lord unless first they tear down the altars they've built to the false gods they worship. Our God is a jealous God (Ex. 20:5) and will not share His glory or our love with another. Gideon had privately built his own altar to the Lord (Judg. 6:24), but now he had to take his public stand, and he had to do it without compromise. Before he could declare war on Midian, he had to declare war on Baal.

—*Be Available*, page 66

9. Why did the men of the city want to kill Gideon? What did God's law have to say about this situation? (See Deut. 13:6–9.) What was likely going through Gideon's mind when he was being confronted about his actions? Where was God during this time?

## From the Commentary

The Midianites and their allies made their annual invasion about that time as more than 135,000 men (Judg. 8:10; 7:12) moved into the Valley of Jezreel. It was time for Gideon to act, and the Spirit of God gave him the wisdom and power that he needed (Judg. 3:10; 11:29; 13:25; 14:6, 19; 15:14). As we seek to do God's will, His Word to us is always, "Not by might, nor by power, but by my spirit" (Zech. 4:6).

When a group of British pastors was discussing the advisability of inviting evangelist D. L. Moody to their city for a crusade, one man asked, "Why must it be Moody? Does D. L. Moody have a monopoly on the Holy Spirit?" Quietly one of the other pastors replied, "No, but it's evident that the Holy Spirit has a monopoly on D. L. Moody."

Gideon blew the trumpet first in his own hometown, and the men of Abiezer rallied behind him. Gideon's reformation in the town had actually accomplished something! Then he sent messengers throughout his own tribe of Manasseh as well as the neighboring tribes of Asher, Zebulun, and Naphtali. These four tribes were near the Valley of Jezreel, and therefore the invading army affected them most. Thus at Gideon's call, 32,000 men responded.

But what chance did 32,000 men have against an army of 135,000 men plus numberless camels (Judg. 7:12)? This is the first mention in the Bible of camels being used in warfare, and certainly they would have given their riders speed and mobility on the battlefield. The Jews were outnumbered and would certainly be outmaneuvered, except for one thing: Jehovah God was on their side, and He had promised them victory.

—*Be Available*, pages 67–68

10. Review Judges 6:33–40. Why did Gideon doubt God's promise? Didn't he have evidence that God was trustworthy? Explain. Why might Gideon have thought he wasn't the best person for the job of leader of the Jewish army? What did Gideon ask God for in order to assure he was the man for the job?

## Looking Inward

Take a moment to reflect on all that you've explored thus far in this study of Judges 6. Review your notes and answers and think about how each of these things matters in your life today.

> *Tips for Small Groups: To get the most out of this section, form pairs or trios and have group members take turns answering these questions. Be honest and as open as you can in this discussion, but most of all, be encouraging and supportive of others. Be sensitive to those who are going through particularly difficult times and don't press for people to speak if they're uncomfortable doing so.*

11. Think of a time when you felt God was allowing "devastation" in your life. What was the devastation? What greater purpose did God have for allowing these things to happen? How have you grown through these circumstances? How do you view God when you think back on that time?

12. What is God preparing you for? What are some of the small victories He's given you that might help you as you face greater challenges? How has your character been affected by the victories (and defeats) God has granted?

13. Have you ever asked God for signs before obeying Him? If so, describe that circumstance. Why did you need a sign from God that what He was asking was the right thing to do? What does this say about your faith? How do you know for certain if God is asking you to do something?

## Going Forward

14. Think of one or two things that you have learned that you'd like to work on in the coming week. Remember that this is all about quality, not quantity. It's better to work on one specific area of life and do it well than to work on many and do poorly (or to be so overwhelmed that you simply don't try).

Do you want to learn how to better trust God when He asks you to do a difficult thing? Be specific. Go back through Judges 6 and put a star next to the phrase or verse that is most encouraging to you. Consider memorizing this verse.

*Real-Life Application Ideas: Consider the most daunting task you have before you this week. This is the one thing you know God wants you to do, but you've hesitated. Perhaps it's committing to a role at church or talking to a neighbor or coworker about your faith. Or maybe it's something even bigger—like finally going on that mission trip or quitting your job to serve in a new and different way. Before you dive into that task, collect all the wisdom you can from friends and Scripture and church leaders and prayer. Rather than asking God for a sign, ask God to give you direction as you seek out those resources, so you can make the best decision possible, trusting God's love for you to fill in the gaps between uncertainty and action. Then ... act.*

## Seeking Help

15. Write a prayer below (or simply pray one in silence), inviting God to work on your mind and heart in those areas you've noted in the Going Forward section. Be honest about your desires and fears.

*Notes for Small Groups:*

- *Look for ways to put into practice the things you wrote in the Going Forward section. Talk with other group members about your ideas and commit to being accountable to one another.*

- *During the coming week, ask the Holy Spirit to continue to reveal truth to you from what you've read and studied.*

- *Before you start the next lesson, read Judges 7—8. For more in-depth lesson preparation, read chapters 5 and 6, "Faith Is the Victory" and "Win the War, Lose the Victory," in* Be Available.

# Victories
## (JUDGES 7—8)

*Before you begin …*
- *Pray for the Holy Spirit to reveal truth and wisdom as you go through this lesson.*
- *Read Judges 7—8. This lesson references chapters 5 and 6 in* Be Available. *It will be helpful for you to have your Bible and a copy of the commentary available as you work through this lesson.*

## Getting Started

### From the Commentary

A faith that can't be tested can't be trusted. Too often, what people think is faith is really only a "warm, fuzzy feeling" about faith or perhaps just "faith in faith." I recall being in a board meeting of an international ministry when one of the board members said enthusiastically, "We're simply going to have to step out by faith!" Quietly another board member asked, "Whose faith?" That question made all of us search our hearts.

J. G. Stipe said, "Faith is like a toothbrush: Everybody should have one and use it regularly, but it isn't safe to use somebody else's." We can sing loudly about the "Faith of Our Fathers," but we can't exercise the faith of our fathers. We can follow men and women of faith and share in their exploits, but we can't succeed in our own personal lives by depending on somebody else's faith.

God tests our faith for at least two reasons: first, to show us whether our faith is real or counterfeit, and second, to strengthen our faith for the tasks He's set before us. I've noticed in my own life and ministry that God has often put us through the valley of testing before allowing us to reach the mountain peak of victory. Spurgeon was right when he said that the promises of God shine brightest in the furnace of affliction, and it is in claiming those promises that we gain the victory.

God tested Gideon's faith by sifting his army of 32,000 volunteers until only 300 men were left. If Gideon's faith had been in the size of his army, then his faith would have been very weak by the time God was through with them! Less than 1 percent of the original 32,000 ended up following Gideon to the battlefield. The words of Winston Churchill concerning the RAF in World War II certainly apply to Gideon's 300: "Never in the field of human conflict was so much owed by so many to so few."

—*Be Available*, pages 74–75

1. What reason did God give Gideon for decreasing the size of the army? What message does this send about God's power? About faith?

*More to Consider: Too often, we're like King Uzziah, who was "greatly helped, until he became powerful. But after Uzziah became powerful, his pride led to his downfall" (2 Chron. 26:15–16). How are people who live by faith better prepared to do God's work? How does knowing our weaknesses give us opportunity to do great things for God? (See 2 Cor. 12:10.)*

2. Choose one verse or phrase from Judges 7—8 that stands out to you. This could be something you're intrigued by, something that makes you uncomfortable, something that puzzles you, something that resonates with you, or just something you want to examine further. Write that here.

# Going Deeper

## From the Commentary

God put Gideon's surviving 10,000 men through a second test by asking them all to take a drink down at the river. *We never know when God is testing us in some ordinary experience of life.* I heard about one leading minister who always took a drive with a prospective pastoral staff member *in the other man's car,* just to see if the car was neat and if the man drove carefully. Whether or not neatness and careful driving habits are always a guarantee of ministerial success is debatable, but the lesson is worth considering. More than one prospective employee has ruined his or her chances for a job while having lunch with the boss, not realizing they were being evaluated. "Make every occasion a great occasion, for you can never tell when somebody may be taking your measure for a larger place." That was said by a man named Marsden, and I've had the quotation, now yellow with age, under the glass on my desk for many years. Pondering it from time to time has done me good.

—*Be Available,* page 76

3. Why did God put Gideon's men through a second test? What significance was there in the two different ways the men drank from the river? What does this suggest about God's relationship with Gideon and his army? What does it say about God's love for them?

*From the Commentary*

The Lord wanted Gideon and his 300 men to attack the camp of Midian that night, but first He had to deal with the fear that still persisted in Gideon's heart. God had already told Gideon three times that He would give Israel victory (6:14, 16; 7:7), and He had reassured him by giving him three special signs: fire from the rock (6:19–21), the wet fleece (6:36–38), and the dry fleece (6:39–40). After all this divine help, Gideon should have been strong in his faith, but such was not the case.

How grateful we should be that God understands us and doesn't condemn us because we have doubts and fears! He keeps giving us wisdom and doesn't scold us when we keep asking (James 1:5). Our great High Priest in heaven sympathizes with our weaknesses (Heb. 4:14–16) and keeps giving us more grace (James 4:6). God remembers that we're only dust (Ps. 103:14) and flesh (78:39).

—*Be Available*, page 78

4. What were two ways God encouraged Gideon's faith (Judg. 7:9; 7:10–14)? What helped Gideon become both confident and courageous in his faith? How is this different from an arrogant faith?

## From the Commentary

> "But without faith it is impossible to please Him, for he who comes to God must believe that He is, and that He is a rewarder of those who diligently seek Him" (Heb. 11:6 NKJV). Faith means more than simply trusting God; it also means *seeking* God and wanting to *please* Him. We don't trust God just to get Him to do things for us. We trust Him because it brings joy to His heart when His children rely on Him, seek Him, and please Him.
>
> How did God reward Gideon's faith?
>
> **God gave him wisdom to prepare the army (Judg. 7:15b–18).**
>
> **God gave him courage to lead the army (Judg. 7:19–22).**
>
> **God gave him opportunity to enlarge the army (Judg. 7:23–25).**
>
> —*Be Available*, pages 80–81

5. Review Judges 7:15–25. What does God's activity here teach us about how God can accomplish His purposes in today's church? How does this go against the common thinking that a "big church" is needed to have a "big impact" in the world? What are some other biblical accounts that teach this same message?

*From the Commentary*

> Thus far in our study of Gideon's life, we've seen his responses to the Lord's call to defeat the enemy. At first Gideon was full of questions and doubts; but then he grew in his faith, believed God's promises, and led his army to victory. In Judges 8, the account focuses on Gideon's responses to various people *after he had won the battle*, and it tells us how he handled some difficult situations.
>
> The chronology in chapter 8 seems to be as follows: Gideon's pursuit of the two kings (vv. 4–12); his disciplining of the defiant Jews on his journey home (vv. 13–17); the protest of the Ephraimites after he arrived home (vv. 1–3); the slaying of the kings (vv. 18–21); and Gideon's "retirement" (vv. 22–35).
>
> —*Be Available*, pages 85–86

6. Review Judges 8:4–35. What challenges did Gideon face after his victory? How did he handle each challenge? What role did God play in each of his challenges (and how he responded)?

## From the Commentary

> The purpose of 8:1–3 is somewhat of a puzzle. It's not likely that the men of Ephraim would complain to Gideon while they were capturing Oreb and Zeeb (7:24–25) and while he was pursuing Zebah and Zalmunna (8:12). Fighting the enemy would have consumed all their energy and attention, and Gideon's reply in verse 3 indicates that the men of Ephraim had already captured and killed Oreb and Zeeb. Perhaps a delegation from the tribe waited on Gideon when the spoils of war were being distributed after he returned home, and that's when they complained.
>
> Knowing that they were a large and important tribe, second only to Judah, the Ephraimites were a proud people. Gideon was from Manasseh, the "brother" tribe to Ephraim, and Ephraim was insulted because he didn't call them to the battle. But why would such an important tribe want to follow a farmer into battle? They had assisted Ehud (3:26–29) and Deborah and Barak (5:13–14), but that was no guarantee they would help Gideon.
>
> —*Be Available*, page 86

7. In what ways was Gideon wise not to call for volunteers from the proud tribe of Ephraim during the attack on Midian? If Gideon had called them and then sent most of them back, how might that have created an even bigger problem? What does this teach us about the importance of carefully thinking through our plans before announcing them?

## From the Commentary

Gideon and his men were pursuing two of the Midianite kings, Zebah and Zalmunna, knowing that if they captured and killed them, the enemy's power would be crippled and eventually broken. The army crossed over the Jordan to Succoth in Gad, hoping to find some nourishment, but the men of Succoth wouldn't help their own brothers. The two and a half tribes that occupied the land east of the Jordan didn't feel as close to the other tribes as they should have, and Gad had sent no soldiers to help either Deborah and Barak (5:17) or Gideon. While others were risking their lives, the people of Gad were doing nothing.

The Ammonites and Moabites, relatives of the Jews through Lot, failed to help Israel with food, and God declared war on them (Deut. 23:3–6). Hospitality is one of the basic laws of the East, and custom demands that the people meet the needs of strangers as well as relatives. Hospitality was also an important ministry in the early church, for there were no hotels where guests might stay, and in times of persecution, many visitors were fleeing (Rom. 12:13; 1 Tim. 5:10; Heb. 13:2; 1 Peter 4:9). Indeed, helping a hungry brother is an opportunity to help the Lord Jesus (Matt. 25:34–40).

*—Be Available*, page 88

8. Review Judges 8:14–17. Why were the men of Succoth skeptical of Gideon's ability to defeat the fleeing Midianite army? How were they impudent in the way they spoke to Gideon? What does this say about the men of Succoth? What was Gideon's response? What does this reveal about Gideon?

## From the Commentary

When Gideon arrived back home at Ophrah, leading Zebah and Zalmunna captive, the procession must have been as exciting as a ticker-tape parade. Gideon was a true hero. With only 300 men, he had routed the enemy camp and then pursued the fleeing soldiers across the Jordan and as far south as Karkor. He had brought his royal prisoners back, plus whatever spoils the men had gathered along the way.

Gideon had a personal matter to settle with these two kings because they had been guilty of killing his brothers at Tabor. The text doesn't tell us when this wicked act took place, but it must have occurred during one of the previous annual Midianite raids. How Gideon's brothers became involved and why they were killed isn't explained to us, but the suggestion is that the act was an unconscionable one.

According to Mosaic law, the family was to avenge crimes like this by killing those responsible for the murder. There was no police system in the land, and each family was expected to track down and punish those who had murdered their relatives, provided the culprit was guilty (Num. 35:9–34). In the case of Zebah and Zalmunna, the culprits were not only murderers but also enemies of Israel.

—*Be Available*, pages 89–90

9. Review Judges 8:18–21. How were the two kings shrewd in the way they answered Gideon? Why did they resort to flattery? What was Gideon's response to this flattery? What impression of him did you get in this episode?

*More to Consider: In those days, how a soldier died was important to his reputation. Abimelech didn't want to die at the hand of a woman (Judg. 9:53–54), and King Saul didn't want to fall into the hands of the Philistines (1 Sam. 31:1–6). Why was this the case? Why was the fear of being humiliated, even in death, so important to the people? How did Gideon help the kings avoid humiliation?*

## From the Commentary

The narrative focuses on two requests, one from the people to Gideon and the other from Gideon to the people.

**(1) The people request a king (Judg. 8:22–23, 29–32).** So popular was Gideon that the people asked him to set up a dynasty, something altogether new for the nation of Israel. This was one way they could reward Gideon for what he had done for them. But it was also somewhat of a guarantee that there would be a measure of unity among the tribes as well as the kind of leadership that would mobilize them against possible future invaders.

Their request was a confession of unbelief, for as Gideon reminded them, *God* was their king.

**(2) Gideon requests gold (Judg. 8:24–28).** The people were only too eager to share their spoils with Gideon. After all, he had brought peace to the land (v. 28) and had refused to become their king. Therefore, it was only right that he receive something for his labors. The Midianites wore gold crescents, either on the ear or the nose (Gen.

24:47), and the Israelite soldiers would have quickly taken these valuable items as they gathered the spoils. Gideon ended up with over forty pounds of gold, plus the wealth he took from Zebah and Zalmunna. No wonder he was able to live like a king!

—*Be Available*, pages 91–92

10. Why did Gideon reject the people's request that he set up a dynasty? Why did Gideon request gold? What do these requests reveal about the people and their relationship with God? About Gideon's relationship with God?

## Looking Inward

Take a moment to reflect on all that you've explored thus far in this study of Judges 7—8. Review your notes and answers and think about how each of these things matters in your life today.

*Tips for Small Groups: To get the most out of this section, form pairs or trios and have group members take turns answering these questions. Be honest and as open as you can in this discussion, but most of all, be encouraging and supportive of others. Be sensitive to those who are going through particularly difficult times and don't press for people to speak if they're uncomfortable doing so.*

11. Have you ever felt that God was "decreasing the size of your army" when you faced a challenge? If so, what prompted that feeling? Why might God have apparently taken something from you that you thought you needed? What did you learn from that situation?

12. Describe a time when announcing your plans before thinking them through led to a problem. Why is it important to think before you act? How can God be a part of that thinking process?

13. Have you ever made a bad decision because someone influenced you with flattery? Explain. Why is it dangerous to listen to flattery? What is a humble and godly response to someone who is trying to change your mind with apparently kind words?

## Going Forward

14. Think of one or two things that you have learned that you'd like to work on in the coming week. Remember that this is all about quality, not quantity. It's better to work on one specific area of life and do it well than to work on many and do poorly (or to be so overwhelmed that you simply don't try).

Do you want to strengthen your faith in God and His leaders? Be specific. Go back through Judges 7—8 and put a star next to the phrase or verse that is most encouraging to you. Consider memorizing this verse.

*Real-Life Application Ideas: Think about a recent success or victory in life. This could be work related, or something you accomplished at home or in the community. Perhaps you got a promotion or you solved a family crisis or you helped a neighbor put in a garden. Whatever the success, think about how you responded to it. Did you celebrate? Did you take ownership of the victory? Did you consider God's role in the success? Spend some time in prayer, asking God to give you wisdom on the proper response to victories in your life. Ask Him to help you respond in a way that glorifies Him. If you want to test yourself to see if you're doing this well, invite feedback from friends and leaders. Then listen to their wisdom and learn from it for the next victory.*

## Seeking Help

15. Write a prayer below (or simply pray one in silence), inviting God to work on your mind and heart in those areas you've noted in the Going Forward section. Be honest about your desires and fears.

*Notes for Small Groups:*

- *Look for ways to put into practice the things you wrote in the Going Forward section. Talk with other group members about your ideas and commit to being accountable to one another.*

- *During the coming week, ask the Holy Spirit to continue to reveal truth to you from what you've read and studied.*

- *Before you start the next lesson, read Judges 9—12. For more in-depth lesson preparation, read chapters 7 and 8, "My Kingdom Come" and "Local Reject Makes Good," in* Be Available.

# Kingdom Come
## (JUDGES 9—12)

*Before you begin …*
- *Pray for the Holy Spirit to reveal truth and wisdom as you go through this lesson.*
- *Read Judges 9—12. This lesson references chapters 7 and 8 in* Be Available. *It will be helpful for you to have your Bible and a copy of the commentary available as you work through this lesson.*

## Getting Started

### From the Commentary

Abimelech was the son of Gideon by a slave woman who lived with her father's family in Shechem (8:30–31; 9:18). His name means "my father is a king." Although Gideon had certainly lived like a king, he had still refused to establish a dynasty in Israel, but Abimelech felt that his father had made a mistake. After his father's death, Abimelech decided that *he* should be king; thus he moved from Ophrah to Shechem, where he started his campaign.

In what he did, Abimelech broke several of God's laws and as a result brought destruction to himself and trouble to the people.

"You shall not covet" is the last of the Ten Commandments (Ex. 20:17 NKJV), but breaking it is the first step toward breaking the other nine. Of itself ambition isn't an evil thing, provided it's mixed with genuine humility and is controlled by the will of God. If it's God's wind that lifts you and you're soaring on wings that He's given you, then fly as high as He takes you. But if you manufacture both the wind and the wings, you're heading for a terrible fall.

"One can never consent to creep when one feels an impulse to soar," said Helen Keller; and her counsel is good, so long as the impulse to soar comes from the Lord. Selfish ambition destroys. "I will ascend into heaven!" turned an angel into the Devil (Isa. 14:13 NKJV), and "Is not this great Babylon, that I have built" turned a king into an animal (Dan. 4:28–37 NKJV). If we exalt ourselves, God has many ways of bringing us down (Matt. 23:12).

"You shall have no other gods before Me" and "You shall not make for yourself a carved image" are the first and second of the Ten Commandments (Ex. 20:3–4 NKJV), and Abimelech broke them both. It's obvious that he was his own god and that he had no interest in God's will for the nation. His accepting money from the Baal worshippers to finance his crusade was a public announcement that he had renounced the God of Israel and was on the side of Baal.

—*Be Available*, pages 97–99

1. Review Judges 9:1–5. What were Abimelech's gods? How did he bow down to might and power? What was his evil plot against his half brothers? What does this reveal about his heart? His greed?

2. Choose one verse or phrase from Judges 9—12 that stands out to you. This could be something you're intrigued by, something that makes you uncomfortable, something that puzzles you, something that resonates with you, or just something you want to examine further. Write that here.

## Going Deeper

*From the Commentary*

The sixth commandment, "You shall not murder" (Ex. 20:13 NKJV), was violated scores of times by Abimelech and his mercenaries, beginning in Ophrah with their slaughter of sixty-nine of Abimelech's seventy half brothers. Why didn't somebody stop these murderers and defend Gideon's family? Because the people of Israel had forgotten both the goodness of the Lord and the kindness of Gideon (Judg. 8:33–35). They had neither the conviction to be concerned nor the courage to intervene. It doesn't take long for society to change yesterday's hero into today's scoundrel. What the Irish poet William Butler Yeats described in his famous poem "The Second Coming" was true in the nation of Israel: The best lack all conviction, while the worst are full of passionate intensity.

"Woe to him who builds a city with bloodshed and establishes a town by crime!" (Hab. 2:12 NIV). Revelation 21:8 and 22:15 make it clear that murderers go to hell. Of course, a murderer can call on the Lord and be saved just as any other sinner can, but there's no evidence that Abimelech and his crowd ever repented of their sins. Their feet were "swift to shed blood" (Rom. 3:15; Isa. 59:7), and the blood that they shed eventually came back on their own heads.

Murder is bad enough, but when brother kills brother, the sin is even more heinous. By murdering his half brothers, Abimelech joined the ranks of other men in the Bible who committed fratricide, including Cain (Gen. 4), Absalom (2 Sam. 13:23ff.), and Jehoram (2 Chron. 21:4). Not very nice company.

—*Be Available*, pages 99–100

3. In what ways did Abimelech break the third commandment? (See Ex. 20:7.) How did he break the ninth commandment? (See Ex. 20:16.) Why does the Bible show us so much of Abimelech's evil ways? In what ways is his story a cautionary tale? What lessons can we take away from his story?

*More to Consider: Read Judges 9:7–21. This is the first parable recorded in Scripture. Besides this "parable of the trees," the Old Testament also contains Nathan's "parable of the ewe lamb" (2 Sam. 12:1–4), the parable by the woman of Tekoa (2 Sam. 14:5–20), the parable of the thistle (2 Kings 14:8–14), and the parable of the vineyard (Isa. 5:1–7). The prophecies of Jeremiah and Ezekiel contain both standard parables as well as "action" parables (Jer. 13; 18—19; 27—28; Ezek. 4—5; 16; 31; etc.). Why were parables such a common form of teaching even in Old Testament times? How did Jesus use the same form to teach the disciples?*

## From the Commentary

After three years of relative success, Abimelech found himself in trouble. It's one thing to acquire a throne and quite something else to defend and retain it. The citizens of Shechem, who had helped crown him king, began to give him trouble, as well as an intruder named Gaal. All of this was from the Lord, who was about to punish both Abimelech and the men of Shechem for the slaughter of Gideon's sons. "Though the mills of God grind slowly, yet they grind exceeding small" (Longfellow, "Retribution").

The activities of at least three days are described in this section.

**Day one—the boasting of Gaal (Judg. 9:25–33).** The Lord created a breech between the king and his followers, so much so that the Shechemites started to work against the king. They began to rob the caravans that passed by the city on the nearby trade routes.

Into this volatile situation stepped a newcomer, Gaal the son of Ebed, a man who knew a good opportunity when he saw it. In a short time, he gained the confidence of the men of Shechem, who were already unhappy with their king, and when a crowd was gathered to celebrate a harvest festival, Gaal openly criticized Abimelech's administration.

**Day two—the defeat of Gaal (Judg. 9:34–41).** Abimelech used some of Gideon's strategy (v. 34), although he didn't have Gideon's faith or the weapons Gideon and his men used.

**Day three—the punishment of Shechem (Judg. 9:42–49).** Abimelech had one more score to settle, and that was with the citizens of Shechem who had cursed him (v. 27) and were attacking the caravans and robbing him of both money and reputation.

—*Be Available*, pages 103–5

4. Compare Abimelech's approach to conflict with Gideon's. What made Gideon's approach stand out? What did Abimelech do to make sure the city didn't rebel against him? What does this reveal about his heart? His fear?

*From the Commentary*

The shedding of innocent blood is something that God takes very seriously and eventually avenges (Deut. 19:10, 13; 21:9; 1 Kings 2:31; Prov. 6:16–17; Isa. 59:7; Jer. 7:6; 22:3, 17; Joel 3:19).

Abimelech paid for the murders he committed, and it happened while he was attempting to protect his throne. Since the people in the city of Thebez, about ten miles from Shechem, had apparently joined in the general rebellion against Abimelech, he went there with his army to punish them as well. Like the people from Beth-Millo, the citizens of Thebez fled to their tower; and Abimelech tried to use the same method of attack that he used so successfully at Shechem.

However, he made the mistake of getting too close to the tower, and a woman dropped an upper millstone on his head and killed him.

—*Be Available*, pages 105–6

5. How was the curse pronounced by Jotham fulfilled? (See Judg. 9:20; Ps. 34:21; Prov. 21:12.) In what ways did Abimelech "get what he deserved"? What made Abimelech's death especially disgraceful, culturally speaking? (See 2 Sam. 11:21.)

## From the Commentary

Life and literature are filled with the "Cinderella legend," stories about rejected people who were eventually "discovered" and elevated to places of honor and authority. Horatio Alger wrote over one hundred boys' novels that focused on the "rags-to-riches" theme, and he became one of the most influential American writers of the last half of the nineteenth century. Whether it's Abraham Lincoln going "from log cabin to White House" or Joseph from the prison to the throne of Egypt, the story of the successful "underdog" is one that will always be popular. We like to see losers become winners.

The account of Jephthah, the main character in Judges 10—12, is that kind of a story, except that it doesn't end with the hero living "happily ever after." After Jephthah's great victory over the Ammonites and Philistines, he experienced anything but happiness, and the narrative ends on a tragic note. The story can be divided into four scenes. The first is all about a nation in decay.

—*Be Available*, page 109

6. What evidence does Judges 10:1–18 give that reveals a nation in spiritual decay? What does spiritual decay look like? How can a nation's citizens resist or even reverse spiritual decay?

*From the Commentary*

In 11:1–29, 32–33 we are introduced to Jephthah, the
man God chose to lead Israel to victory. What kind of
man was he?

Jephthah wasn't to blame for his birth. His father, Gilead,
had only one wife, but he consorted with a prostitute and
fathered a son. At least Gilead acknowledged the boy and
took him into his home, but his other sons didn't accept
this "son of a strange woman." When Gilead died and the
inheritance was to be divided, the legitimate sons drove
Jephthah away. Little did they realize they were rejecting
a future judge of Israel.

Jephthah's brothers didn't want him, but the elders of
Israel needed him and sent a deputation eighty miles to
the land of Tob to ask him to take charge. Jephthah's
reply sounds a good deal like what the Lord had said to
the people when they turned to Him for help (10:13–14).
Apparently the Jewish leaders had cooperated with
Gilead's sons in expelling the unwanted brother from the
land, but Jephthah listened to them and made sure their
offer was valid. He was willing to lead them against the
enemy if the elders would name him ruler of Gilead.

—*Be Available*, pages 113–14

7. What is significant about Jephthah's birth and youth? What does this
reveal about how God chooses His leaders? What can we learn about God's
grace? His sovereignty?

*From the Commentary*

Before declaring war, Jephthah tried peaceful negotiations with the Ammonites, but the negotiations failed. Nevertheless, this section does tell us two things about Jephthah: (1) He knew the Scriptures and the history of his people, and (2) he was not a hothead who was looking for a fight. Being a military man himself, Jephthah knew that a war could result in thousands of Jewish men being killed, and he wanted to avoid that if at all possible.

The king of Ammon declared that he and his men were only reclaiming land that the Jews, under the leadership of Moses, had stolen from them. If Israel would restore that land, he would call off his troops. But Jephthah presented four compelling arguments that should have convinced the Ammonites that they were wrong.

First, he presented the facts of history (Judg. 11:14–22). His second argument was that the Lord had given Israel the land (vv. 23–24). Jephthah's third argument was that Israel had lived on the land for centuries (vv. 25–26). Jephthah's final argument was that the Ammonites were actually fighting against the Lord (vv. 27–28).

—*Be Available*, pages 115–16

8. Why didn't Jephthah's arguments convince the Ammonites they were wrong? By what authority did Jephthah call for volunteers to muster his army? (See Judg. 3:10; 6:34.) What bargain did he make with God? What was the result of that bargain?

*More to Consider: The writer of Hebrews wrote that Jephthah was a man of faith and his victory was a victory of faith (Heb. 11:32–33). What does this tell us about the relationship between a person's birth and his or her God-given purpose? In his message to the king of Ammon, Jephthah revealed his knowledge of the Word of God, and this Word was the source of his faith. Read Romans 10:17 and 1 John 5:4. How do these verses speak to the role faith played in Jephthah's story?*

## From the Commentary

While going out to battle, Jephthah made a vow to the Lord. It was certainly acceptable to God for the Jews to make vows, provided they obeyed the laws that He had given through Moses to govern the use of vows (Lev. 27; Num. 30; Deut. 23:21–25). Vows were completely voluntary, but the Lord expected the people to fulfill them (Eccl. 5:1–6).

Jephthah's vow was really a bargain with the Lord: If God would give the Israelites victory over the Ammonites, Jephthah would sacrifice to the Lord whatever came out of his house when he arrived home in Mizpeh. God did give him victory, and Jephthah kept his promise.

—*Be Available*, page 117

9. What happened to Jephthah's daughter? Was Jephthah's vow wise or rash? Why? In spite of Numbers 30:1–2, would God take seriously a vow

that violated both human rights and divine law? Would a Spirit-empowered man (Judg. 11:29) committed to the Lord (11:11) even make such a vow? What do all of these questions suggest about the story behind Jephthah's words in 11:35?

## From the Commentary

The leaders of the tribe of Ephraim expressed to Jephthah the same pride and anger they had shown to Gideon (8:1). As before, they wanted to share the glory of the victory, but they hadn't been too eager to risk their lives in the battle. The men of Ephraim were so angry that they threatened to burn Jephthah's house down. They had absolutely no respect for the new ruler of the Transjordanic tribes.

Gideon had pacified the Ephraimites with flattery, but Jephthah took a more direct approach. To begin with, he reminded them that his first concern was to defeat the Ammonites, not to please his neighbors. Second, during the eighteen years Ammon had oppressed the people of Gilead, nobody from Ephraim had offered to come to their rescue. Third, Jephthah had issued a call for the tribes to assist him in his attack on the enemy, but Ephraim hadn't responded. Without their help, the Lord gave Jephthah and his army victory, so the proud Ephraimites (who didn't like being left out) had nothing to complain about.

Perhaps Jephthah should have practiced Proverbs 15:1 and 17:14 and avoided a war, but then, maybe it was time somebody called Ephraim's bluff and taught them a lesson. The men of Ephraim resorted to name-calling and taunted the Gileadites by calling them "renegades from Ephraim and Manasseh" (Judg. 12:4 NIV). Actually, the tribes east of the Jordan River—Reuben, Gad, and half of the tribe of Manasseh—had been granted their land by Moses and Joshua (Num. 32; Josh. 22). Thus the words of the Ephraimites were an insult to the Lord and His servants.

—*Be Available*, pages 120–21

10. How is the violence in this story an example of people refusing to accept logical reasoning and confessing their faults? How is this similar to the core cause of most family disagreements, church battles, and international conflicts? (See James 4:1–12.)

## Looking Inward

Take a moment to reflect on all that you've explored thus far in this study of Judges 9—12. Review your notes and answers and think about how each of these things matters in your life today.

*Tips for Small Groups: To get the most out of this section, form pairs or trios and have group members take turns answering these questions. Be honest and as open as you can in this discussion, but most of all, be encouraging and supportive of others. Be sensitive to those who are going through particularly difficult times and don't press for people to speak if they're uncomfortable doing so.*

11. Take a moment to think about the commandments you've broken. What have you learned since then to help you understand why God's commandments are valid, even considering Jesus' role in bringing a new message of grace? What can we learn about God from the Ten Commandments? How can you apply that wisdom to growing your faith and relationship with Him today?

12. Describe a time when you went through spiritual decay. What caused the decay? How did you find your way back to a place of spiritual health?

13. Have you ever felt like Jephthah must have early in his life (unwanted, unloved by family or friends)? How can the way God used him inspire and encourage you when you're feeling inadequate or unloved? What are some ways God has already used you for great things?

## Going Forward

14. Think of one or two things that you have learned that you'd like to work on in the coming week. Remember that this is all about quality, not quantity. It's better to work on one specific area of life and do it well than to work on many and do poorly (or to be so overwhelmed that you simply don't try).

Do you want to learn how to live honorably and humbly after experiencing success? Be specific. Go back through Judges 9—12 and put a star next to the phrase or verse that is most encouraging to you. Consider memorizing this verse.

*Real-Life Application Ideas: In Jephthah's story, a life of doing God's will didn't result in a particularly happy ending. Think about some of the chapters in your story so far that could lead you to a less-than-happy ending. Then consider how God can use even those chapters to accomplish His will in your life. Take some time to think about what it means to have a "happy ending" in life. What does that look like to the world? What does that look like to God? Take steps to make sure you're moving toward a happy ending in God's economy, whether or not that lines up with one the world would say is happy.*

## Seeking Help

15. Write a prayer below (or simply pray one in silence), inviting God to work on your mind and heart in those areas you've noted in the Going Forward section. Be honest about your desires and fears.

*Notes for Small Groups:*

- *Look for ways to put into practice the things you wrote in the Going Forward section. Talk with other group members about your ideas and commit to being accountable to one another.*

- *During the coming week, ask the Holy Spirit to continue to reveal truth to you from what you've read and studied.*

- *Before you start the next lesson, read Judges 13—16. For more in-depth lesson preparation, read chapters 9 and 10, "The Light That Flickered" and "The Light That Failed," in* Be Available.

# Two Lights
## (JUDGES 13—16)

*Before you begin …*
- *Pray for the Holy Spirit to reveal truth and wisdom as you go through this lesson.*
- *Read Judges 13—16. This lesson references chapters 9 and 10 in* Be Available. *It will be helpful for you to have your Bible and a copy of the commentary available as you work through this lesson.*

## Getting Started

*From the Commentary*

Consider the great promise that was wrapped up in this person named Samson.

He had a nation to protect (Judg. 13:1). With monotonous regularity we've read this phrase in the book of Judges (3:7, 12; 4:1–2; 6:1; 10:6–7), and here it appears for the last time. It introduces the longest period of oppression that God sent to His people, forty years of Philistine domination.

The Philistines were among the "sea people" who, in the twelfth century BC, migrated from an area of Greece to the coastal plain of Canaan. The Jews weren't able to occupy that territory during their conquest of the land (Josh. 13:1–2). As you study your map, you'll note that their national life focused around the five key cities of Ashdod, Gaza, Ashkelon, Gath, and Ekron (1 Sam. 6:17). The land between Israel's hill country and the coastal plain was called the "Shephelah," which means "low country," and it separated Philistia from Israel. Samson was born in Zorah, a city in Dan near the Philistine border, and he often crossed that border either to serve God or satisfy his appetites.

Samson judged Israel "in the days of the Philistines" (Judg. 15:20), which means that his twenty years in office were *during* the forty years of Philistine rule. Dr. Leon Wood dates the beginning of the Philistine oppression about 1095 BC and the end in 1055 BC with Israel's victory at Mizpeh (1 Sam. 7). About the middle of this period the battle of Aphek occurred when Israel was ignominiously defeated by the Philistines and lost the ark and three priests (1 Sam. 4). Dr. Wood suggests that Samson's judgeship started about the time of the tragedy at Aphek and that his main job was to harass the Philistines and keep them from successfully overrunning the land and menacing the people.

—*Be Available*, pages 126–27

1. Why is it notable that there is no evidence that Israel cried out to God for deliverance at any time during the forty years of Philistine domination? (See 1 Sam. 13:11–14.) What does Judges 15:9–13 indicate about the Jews' apparent contentment? Why wouldn't they have wanted Samson to "rock the boat"?

*More to Consider: Unlike most of the previous judges, Samson didn't deliver his people from foreign domination, but he began the work of deliverance that others would finish (13:5). How did Samson's unpredictability as a hero affect the way the Philistines reacted to him? (See 16:24.) How did he keep them from devastating Israel? Read 1 Samuel 7 and 2 Samuel 5:17–25. What do these verses tell us about the roles Samuel and David played in giving Israel complete victory over the Philistines?*

2. Choose one verse or phrase from Judges 13—16 that stands out to you. This could be something you're intrigued by, something that makes you uncomfortable, something that puzzles you, something that resonates with you, or just something you want to examine further. Write that here.

## Going Deeper

### From the Commentary

Ordinarily, Jewish worshippers had to bring their offerings to the tabernacle altar at Shiloh, but since the "man of God" commanded Manoah to offer the burnt offering, it was permissible to do it there, using a rock as the altar. Suddenly, the visitor ascended to heaven in the flame! Only then did Manoah and his wife discover that their visitor was an angel from the Lord. This frightened Manoah, because the Jews believed that nobody could look upon God and live (Judg. 6:19–23). Using common sense, Manoah's wife convinced him that they couldn't die and fulfill God's promises at the same time.

Every baby born into a godly home carries the responsibility of honoring the family name. Samson's inconsistent life brought shame to his father's house just as it brought shame to the name of the Lord. Samson's relatives had to pull his body out of the wreckage of the Philistine temple and take it home for burial (16:31). In one sense, it was a day of victory over God's enemies, but it was also a day of defeat for Samson's family.

—*Be Available*, page 130

3. Review Judges 13:2–23. What are some of the ways Samson's life brought shame to his father's house? How did God overcome Samson's inconsistencies to accomplish His will anyway? What does this tell us about God?

## From the Commentary

The baby was born and was named Samson, which means "sunny" or "brightness." Certainly he brought light and joy to Manoah and his wife, who thought they would never have a family, and he also began to bring light to Israel during the dark days of Philistine oppression. While other judges were said to be clothed with God's Spirit (3:10; 6:34; 11:29), only of Samson is it said "the LORD blessed him" (13:24; see Luke 1:80 and 2:52). The hand of God was on him in a special way.

The secret of Samson's great strength was his Nazirite vow, symbolized by his unshorn hair (Judg. 16:17), and the source of that strength was the Holy Spirit of God (13:25; 14:6, 19; 15:14). We aren't told that Samson's physique was especially different from that of other men, although he may have resembled the strong men pictured in Bible storybooks. Perhaps it was as he entered his teen years, when a Jewish boy became a "son of the law," that he began to demonstrate his amazing ability.

Only a few of Samson's great feats are recorded in the book of Judges: killing the lion bare-handed (14:5–6); slaying thirty Philistines (v. 19); catching 300 foxes (or jackals) and tying torches to their tails (15:3–5); breaking bonds (15:14; 16:9, 12, 14); slaying 1,000 men with the jawbone of a donkey (15:15); carrying off the Gaza city gate (16:3); and destroying the Philistine building (v. 30). Judges 16:24 indicates that he had done many more

feats than those listed above, feats that had aggravated the
Philistine people.

—*Be Available*, pages 130–31

4. Review Judges 13:24–25. What impression does one get of Samson's life?
In what ways was he a fun-loving character? Did he take himself seriously?
How might this have impacted his effectiveness as a leader?

## From the Commentary

According to Hebrews 11:32, Samson was a man of faith,
but he certainly wasn't a faithful man. He wasn't faithful
to his parents' teaching, his Nazirite vow, or the laws of
the Lord. It didn't take long for Samson to lose almost
everything the Lord had given him, except his great
strength, and he finally lost that as well.

The Lord had given Samson a godly heritage, and he had
been raised to honor the Lord, but when Samson fell in
love, he wouldn't listen to his parents when they warned
him. Samson had wandered four miles into enemy territory where he was captivated by a Philistine woman and

decided to marry her. This, of course, was contrary to God's law (Ex. 34:12–16; Deut. 7:1–3; and see 2 Cor. 6:14–18).

Samson was living by sight and not by faith. He was controlled by "the lust of the eyes" (1 John 2:16) rather than by the law of the Lord. The important thing to Samson was not pleasing the Lord, or even pleasing his parents, but pleasing himself (Judg. 14:3, 7; see 2 Cor. 5:14–15).

When God isn't permitted to rule in our lives, He overrules and works out His will in spite of our decisions. Of course, we're the losers for rebelling against Him, but God will accomplish His purposes either with us or in spite of us (Est. 4:10–14). Samson should have been going to a war instead of to a wedding, but God used this event to give Samson occasion to attack the enemy. Because of this event, Samson killed thirty men (Judg. 14:19), burned up the enemy crops (15:1–5), slaughtered a great number of Philistines (vv. 7–8), and slew 1,000 men (v. 15). Samson hadn't planned these things, but God worked them out just the same.

—*Be Available*, page 132

5. Review Judges 14:1–4. How was Samson both a faithful yet unfaithful man? What does this apparent contradiction say about the role of faith in the life of a believer? What does Samson's story reveal about God's choice of leaders and what He expects of them? What does it say about God's grace?

*From the Commentary*

Since Samson hadn't brought any men with him to serve as "friends of the bridegroom" (Matt. 9:15 NKJV), the Philistines rounded up thirty men to do the job for him. These men may also have served as guards for the Philistines, for Samson's reputation had preceded him, and they were never sure what he would do next. Since the atmosphere must have been tense at the beginning of the feast, Samson sought to liven things up by posing a riddle. Sad to say, he constructed the riddle out of the experience of his sin! He didn't take seriously the fact that he had violated his Nazirite vows. It's bad enough to disobey God, but when you make a joke out of it, you've sunk to new depths of spiritual insensitivity.

It would have been an expensive thing for the thirty guests to supply Samson with sixty garments, so they were desperate to learn the answer to the riddle. Their only recourse was to enlist the help of Samson's wife. Thus they threatened to kill her and burn down her father's house if she didn't supply the answer before the week was up. Samson resolutely refused to tell her, but on the seventh day, he relented. Since the marriage was to be consummated on the seventh day, perhaps that had something to do with it. First the Philistine woman enticed him (Judg. 14:1), then she controlled him (v. 17), and then she betrayed him (v. 17), which is the way the world always treats the compromising believer. Samson could kill lions and break ropes, but he couldn't overcome the power of a woman's tears.

We wonder how his wife felt being compared to a heifer? The proverb simply means, "You couldn't have done what you did if you hadn't broken the rules," because heifers weren't used for plowing. Since the guests had played foul, technically Samson could have refused to pay the prize, but he generously agreed to keep his promise. Perhaps he found out that his wife's life had been threatened and he didn't want to put her and her family into jeopardy again.

Those who can't control their tongue can't control their bodies (James 3:2), and in Samson's case, the consequences of this lack of discipline were disastrous.

—*Be Available*, pages 133–34

6. How would things have been different if Samson had won his way and married a Philistine woman? How can unholy alliances hinder the work of the Lord (2 Cor. 6:14–18)? How would this story have played out differently if Samson had listened first to the Lord?

## From the Commentary

The passion to get even seemed to govern Samson's life. His motto was, "As they did unto me, so have I done unto them" (Judg. 15:11). I realize that as the defender of Israel, Samson's calling was to defeat the enemy, but you long to see him fighting "the battles of the Lord" and not just his own private wars. When David faced the Philistines, he saw them as the enemies of the Lord and sought to honor the name of the Lord in his victory (1 Sam. 17). Samson's attitude was different.

As Christians, we need to beware of hiding selfish motives under the cloak of religious zeal and calling it "righteous indignation." Personal vengeance and private gain rather than the glory of the Lord have motivated more than one "crusader" in the church. What some people think is godly zeal may actually be ungodly anger, fed by pride and motivated by selfishness.

—*Be Available*, pages 139–40

7. How does Samson avenge his ruined marriage? (See Judg. 15:1–5.) How does he avenge his wife's death? (See 15:6–8.) What is the difference between righteous indignation and a religious temper tantrum? (See Eph. 4:26.) Which was Samson acting out?

*From the Commentary*

> When the men of Judah learned that the Philistines wanted only to capture and bind Samson, they offered to help. A nation is in a sad state indeed when the citizens cooperate with the enemy and hand over their own God-appointed leader! This is the only time during Samson's judgeship that the Jews mustered an army, *and it was for the purpose of capturing one of their own men*!
>
> —*Be Available*, page 142

8. Why did Samson decide to give himself up to the army? What was the alternative? In what ways was Samson's decision heroic? Why did the men of Judah miss this?

*More to Consider: Samson had a way with words. At his wedding feast, he devised a clever riddle (14:14), and after this great victory, he wrote a poem. It's based on the similarity between the sounds of the Hebrew words* hamor *("donkey") and* homer *("heap"). James Moffatt renders it: "With the jawbone of an ass I have piled them in a mass. With the jawbone of an ass I have assailed assailants." What does this cleverness teach us about Samson? How might his way with words have served him well in his role as judge? How did they get him into trouble?*

## From the Commentary

Gaza was an important seaport town located about forty miles from Samson's hometown of Zorah. We aren't told why Samson went there, but it's not likely he was looking for sensual pleasure. There were plenty of prostitutes available in Israel even though the law condemned this practice (Lev. 19:29; Deut. 22:21). It was after he arrived in Gaza that Samson saw a prostitute and decided to visit her. Once again the lust of the eyes and the lust of the flesh combined to grip Samson and make him a slave to his passions.

It seems incredible to us that a servant of God (Judg. 15:18), who did great works in the power of the Spirit, would visit a prostitute, but the record is here for all to read. The Lord certainly didn't approve of such behavior, especially on the part of a Nazirite, and the experience was for Samson one more step down into darkness and

destruction. In recent years, there have been enough ministerial scandals in the United States alone to put all of us
on guard. "Therefore let him who thinks he stands take
heed lest he fall" (1 Cor. 10:12 NKJV).

—*Be Available*, page 144

9. Review Judges 16:1–3. Why did Samson tempt himself? What does this
say about his relationship with God? In what ways was Samson his own
worst enemy in this situation? What does it say about God that He was
willing to work through someone like Samson?

*From the Commentary*

How do you assess the life and ministry of a man like
Samson? I think Alexander Maclaren says it well: "Instead
of trying to make a lofty hero out of him, it is far better to
recognize frankly the limitations of his character and the
imperfections of his religion…. If the merely human passion of vengeance throbbed fiercely in Samson's prayer, he
had never heard 'Love your enemies'; and, for his epoch,

the destruction of the enemies of God and of Israel was duty."

His decline began when he disagreed with his parents about marrying a Philistine girl. Then he disdained his Nazirite vow and defiled himself. He disregarded the warnings of God, disobeyed the Word of God, and was defeated by the enemies of God. He probably thought that he had the privilege of indulging in sin since he wore the badge of a Nazirite and won so many victories for the Lord, but he was wrong.

—*Be Available*, pages 149–50

10. Read Proverbs 25:28 and 16:32. How do these verses capture Samson's character? What does Samson's life teach us about temptation? About the lure and danger of power? About God's grace?

## Looking Inward

Take a moment to reflect on all that you've explored thus far in this study of Judges 13—16. Review your notes and answers and think about how each of these things matters in your life today.

*Tips for Small Groups: To get the most out of this section, form pairs or trios and have group members take turns answering these questions. Be honest and as open as you can in this discussion, but most of all, be encouraging and supportive of others. Be sensitive to those who are going through particularly difficult times and don't press for people to speak if they're uncomfortable doing so.*

11. Do you relate to Samson? If so, in what ways? Do you ever wonder if your flaws make it impossible for God to accomplish good things through you? What does Samson's story say to you about that?

12. When has your tongue gotten you in trouble? Why is it so easy for our words to cause harm? What are some practical ways to avoid making the same mistake in the future? Have you ever felt like your words have harmed your relationships with others? With God? If so, how can you repair those relationships?

13. What are some of the ways you've tempted yourself in the past year? How does tempting yourself affect your relationship with God? What are some ways to avoid putting yourself in compromising situations? How can a close community of friends help you avoid temptation?

## Going Forward

14. Think of one or two things that you have learned that you'd like to work on in the coming week. Remember that this is all about quality, not quantity. It's better to work on one specific area of life and do it well than to work on many and do poorly (or to be so overwhelmed that you simply don't try).

Do you want to trust God's direction when you feel tempted to do your own thing? Be specific. Go back through Judges 13—16 and put a star next to the phrase or verse that is most encouraging to you. Consider memorizing this verse.

> *Real-Life Application Ideas: Samson was a walking contradiction—a man of faith who was frequently unfaithful in his earthly relationships. This week, take a close look at how consistent your life is with God's will. Consider the areas where you might "fudge" the truth or situations when you're less than faithful to a friend or family member. How do these choices affect your relationship with God? Begin working on each of these areas as you seek to live for God in all areas of your daily life. But also, be open to God's grace when things don't line up.*

## Seeking Help

15. Write a prayer below (or simply pray one in silence), inviting God to work on your mind and heart in those areas you've noted in the Going Forward section. Be honest about your desires and fears.

*Notes for Small Groups:*

- *Look for ways to put into practice the things you wrote in the Going Forward section. Talk with other group members about your ideas and commit to being accountable to one another.*

- *During the coming week, ask the Holy Spirit to continue to reveal truth to you from what you've read and studied.*

- *Before you start the next lesson, read Judges 17—18. For more in-depth lesson preparation, read chapter 11, "'The Center Cannot Hold,'" in* Be Available.

# The Center
## (JUDGES 17—18)

*Before you begin ...*
- *Pray for the Holy Spirit to reveal truth and wisdom as you go through this lesson.*
- *Read Judges 17—18. This lesson references chapter 11 in* Be Available. *It will be helpful for you to have your Bible and a copy of the commentary available as you work through this lesson.*

## Getting Started

*From the Commentary*

> In his well-known poem "The Second Coming," the Irish poet William Butler Yeats describes the collapse of civilization in vivid and frightening imagery. Each time I read the poem, I feel chilled within, and then I give thanks that I know the One who is coming.
>
> "Things fall apart," writes Yeats; "the center cannot hold."
>
> The closing chapters of the book of Judges echo that

theme: "the center cannot hold." The nation that once marched triumphantly through Canaan to the glory of God now disintegrates morally and politically and brings disgrace to His name. But what else can you expect when there is "no king in Israel" (17:6) and the people are flouting the laws of God?

The events described in chapters 17—21 took place earlier in the period of the judges, probably before the forty-year rule of the Philistines. The movements of the tribe of Dan would have been difficult and the war against Benjamin impossible if the Philistines had been in charge at that time. The writer departed from historical chronology and put these events together as an "appendix" to the book to show how wicked the people had become.

—*Be Available*, page 153

1. What does the people's wickedness look like in these chapters? How were things falling apart in these three areas of life: home, ministry, society? How does this parallel some of our challenges in the world today?

2. Choose one verse or phrase from Judges 17—18 that stands out to you. This could be something you're intrigued by, something that makes you uncomfortable, something that puzzles you, something that resonates with you, or just something you want to examine further. Write that here.

## Going Deeper

*From the Commentary*

God has established three institutions in society: the home, human government, and the worshipping community—Israel under the old covenant and the church under the new covenant. The first of these, in both time and significance, is the home, because the home is the basis for society. When God wedded Adam to Eve in the garden, He laid the foundation for the social institutions humanity would build. When that foundation crumbles, society begins to fall apart. "If the foundations be destroyed, what can the righteous do?" (Ps. 11:3).

Somebody stole 1,100 shekels of silver from Grandmother, and she pronounced a curse on the thief, not knowing that she was cursing her own son. It was the fear of the curse, not the fear of the Lord, that motivated the son to confess his crime and restore the money. Then Grandmother joyfully neutralized the curse by blessing her son. In gratitude for the return of her money, she dedicated part of the silver to the Lord and made an idol out of it. Her son added the new idol to his "god collection" in his house, a "shrine" cared for by one of his sons whom Micah had consecrated as priest.

Have you ever seen a family more spiritually and morally confused than this one? They managed to break almost all of the Ten Commandments (Ex. 20:1–17) *and yet not feel the least bit guilty before the Lord*! In fact, they thought they were serving the Lord by the bizarre things they did!

The son didn't honor his mother; instead, he stole from her and then lied about it. First, he coveted the silver, and then he took it. (According to Col. 3:5, covetousness is idolatry.)

—*Be Available*, page 154

3. How did Micah's mother break the first two commandments? (See Deut. 12:1–14.) Did Micah's mother deal effectively with her son's sins? Explain. How did her character affect the way she acted?

*More to Consider: The name Micah means "Who is like Jehovah." In what ways did he fail to live up to his name?*

## From the Commentary

> Not only did God establish the home and instruct parents how to raise their children (Deut. 6), but He also instituted spiritual leadership in the worshipping community. Under the old covenant, the tabernacle and then the temple were the center of the community, and the Aaronic priesthood supervised both. Under the new covenant, the church of Jesus Christ is the temple of God (Eph. 2:19–22), and the Holy Spirit calls and equips ministers to serve Him and His people (1 Cor. 12–14; Eph. 4:1–16). In His Word, God told the Old Testament priests what they were supposed to do, and in His Word today, the Holy Spirit guides His church and explains its order and its ministry.
>
> —*Be Available*, page 156

4. Review Judges 17:7–13. Why was spiritual leadership such an important aspect of the Israelites' history? How are things similar in today's church? How are they different?

## From Today's World

Churches today host a variety of activities and ministries, some of which are meant to reach out into the community, others of which are meant to bring people into the church. Leadership is always a challenge in ministry, and people with little or no experience are often needed to take on leadership roles. While the Bible proves over and over again that God can use anyone to accomplish His purposes, poor leadership can often result in disaster in the local church.

5. What are the most important character traits for a successful church leader? How can a church use people with various levels of spiritual maturity in leadership and support roles? Why is the spiritual maturity of a leader a key indicator of the success of a program or ministry?

## From the Commentary

A young Levite named Jonathan (Judg. 18:30) set out to find a place to live and work, even if it meant abandoning his calling as a servant of God. The nation was at a low ebb spiritually, and he could have done something to help bring the people back to God. He was only one man, but that's all God needs to begin a great work that can make a difference in the history of a nation. Instead of being available to God, Jonathan was agreeable only to men, and he eventually found himself a comfortable home and job with Micah.

If Jonathan is typical of God's servants in that period of history, then it's no wonder the nation of Israel was confused and corrupt. He had no appreciation for his high calling as a Levite, a chosen servant of God. Not only were the Levites to assist the priests in their ministries (Num. 3:6–13; 8:17–18), but they were also to teach the law to the people (Neh. 8:7–9; 2 Chron. 17:7–9; 35:3) and be involved in the sacred music and the praises of Israel (1 Chron. 23:28–32; Ezra 3:10). Jonathan gave up all that for comfort and security in the home of an idolater.

Jonathan's ministry, however, wasn't a spiritual ministry at all. To begin with, he was a *hireling* and not a true shepherd (Judg. 18:4; John 10:12–13). He didn't serve the true and living God; he worked for Micah and his idols. Jonathan wasn't a spokesperson for the Lord; he gave people just the message they wanted to hear (Judg. 18:6). When he was offered a place involving more money, more people, and more prestige, he took it immediately and gave thanks for it (v. 19). And then he assisted his new employers in stealing his former employer's gods!

—*Be Available*, pages 156–57

6. In ministry, what's the difference between a hired worker and a true shepherd? (See Gal. 1:6–10.) How are people who aren't dedicated to God's mission subject to fall for idols? What are some of the idols people worship

today? What does this teach us about choosing leaders for ministries and evaluating those leaders?

## From the Commentary

> God should have been the king in Israel and His Word the law that governed society, but the people preferred to "do their own thing." If the people had forsaken their idols, and if the elders of Israel had consulted God's law and obeyed it for God's glory, Israel could have been governed successfully. Instead, "Every man did that which was right in his own eyes" (Judg. 21:25), and the result was a society filled with competition and confusion.
>
> —*Be Available*, page 158

7. How did the tribe of Dan suffer from the sin of covetousness? Why was this such a common sin in the early days of the Israelites? What does it say about their faith? About their sense of entitlement? How is that evident in churches even today?

*From the Commentary*

> It was Jonathan's dialect that attracted the attention of the five spies, because he didn't speak quite like a man from Ephraim. When they asked what a Levitical priest was doing in a private home in Ephraim—a very good question, by the way (1 Kings 19:9, 13)—he told them the truth: He was hired to do the job! Since somebody else was paying the bill, the spies thought it was permissible to get "spiritual counsel" from Jonathan, and he told them what they wanted to hear.
>
> —*Be Available*, page 159

8. How was the tribe of Dan rejecting God's counsel by refusing to remain in the land He had assigned to them? How might this have affected the way God then chose to relate to them? (See John 7:17.)

*From the Commentary*

> On their way to capture Laish, the people of Dan paused at Micah's house in Ephraim. The spies told the men that

Micah had a wonderful collection of gods, hinting, of course, that the collection would be valuable to them as they traveled, warred, and established their new home. While the armed men stood at the gate of the city, the five spies, who knew Jonathan, invaded the shrine and stole the gods.

When the five men, with their religious loot, arrived back at the city gate, the priest was shocked to see what they had done. But the Danites silenced him by hiring him, and since he was a hireling, Jonathan was ready for a better offer. The Danites not only broke into Micah's shrine and stole his gods, but they also stole his chaplain. Not a bad day's work!

The Danites put the women and children in the front since that was the safest place, because any attacks would come from the rear. By the time the Danites had traveled some distance away, Micah discovered that his shrine was out of business, having neither gods nor priest; so he called his neighbors together, and they pursued the invaders. After all, a man must protect his gods!

—*Be Available*, page 160

9. Why did Micah have to turn around and go home? What is the significance of his sad question, "What else do I have?" How does this reveal the contrast between religion that is based on idol worship and faith in God, who is not beholden to an idol? (See Isa. 46:1–7.)

*From the Commentary*

> Someone has said that there are only three philosophies of life in today's world: (1) "What's mine is mine, I'll keep it"; (2) "What's yours is mine, I'll take it"; and (3) "What's mine is yours, I'll share it." The Danites followed the second philosophy, and so do too many other grasping people. One of the current booming industries in the United States is the installing of security systems in private homes. The number of shooting sprees in shopping malls and fast-food restaurants has frightened many people into doing their shopping online.
>
> We don't know how many people lived in Laish, but the wanton murders of even a few hundred innocent people is a crime of gross proportions.
>
> —*Be Available*, page 161

10. Why did the Danites follow the second philosophy above? What are some other examples of a people following that philosophy? How does such a way of life often lead to war? How is the third philosophy listed above similar to what Jesus taught? How might the events described in Judges have played out differently if the people had followed the third philosophy more than the first or second?

## Looking Inward

Take a moment to reflect on all that you've explored thus far in this study of Judges 17—18. Review your notes and answers and think about how each of these things matters in your life today.

*Tips for Small Groups: To get the most out of this section, form pairs or trios and have group members take turns answering these questions. Be honest and as open as you can in this discussion, but most of all, be encouraging and supportive of others. Be sensitive to those who are going through particularly difficult times and don't press for people to speak if they're uncomfortable doing so.*

11. What are some of the ways you've been a spiritual leader to others? What are some ways others have led you spiritually? Why is this so important to your relationship with God? With other believers? With nonbelievers?

12. In what ways do you sometimes suffer from the sin of covetousness? How does this play out in your daily life? What is a proper response to the success and wealth of others? What are some ways you can grow closer to God when you feel tempted to covet?

13. Which philosophy do you most follow: what's mine is mine; what's yours is mine; what's mine is yours? Why do you tend to live this way? What would it look like to be more generous in your lifestyle rather than to hold tight to your "stuff"?

## Going Forward

14. Think of one or two things that you have learned that you'd like to work on in the coming week. Remember that this is all about quality, not quantity. It's better to work on one specific area of life and do it well than to work on many and do poorly (or to be so overwhelmed that you simply don't try).

Do you want to identify and let go of the idols in your life? Be specific. Go back through Judges 17—18 and put a star next to the phrase or verse that is most encouraging to you. Consider memorizing this verse.

*Real-Life Application Ideas: This week, take a close look at the idols in your life. It probably won't take long to find the easy ones—money, physical items, success, safety. But look deeper. Some of our most troublesome idols are things that actually look pretty good on the surface. For example, a relationship with a significant other could become an idol—especially if that relationship is more important to you than your relationship with Christ. This doesn't mean that the relationship isn't important, of course, just that it's critical to understand priorities in your faith. As you discover your idols, ask God to help you keep them in perspective, so He is always the primary focus of your life, no matter what.*

## Seeking Help

15. Write a prayer below (or simply pray one in silence), inviting God to work on your mind and heart in those areas you've noted in the Going Forward section. Be honest about your desires and fears.

*Notes for Small Groups:*

- *Look for ways to put into practice the things you wrote in the Going Forward section. Talk with other group members about your ideas and commit to being accountable to one another.*

- *During the coming week, ask the Holy Spirit to continue to reveal truth to you from what you've read and studied.*

- *Before you start the next lesson, read Judges 19—21. For more in-depth lesson preparation, read chapter 12, "War and Peace," in* Be Available.

# War and Peace
## (JUDGES 19—21)

*Before you begin ...*
- *Pray for the Holy Spirit to reveal truth and wisdom as you go through this lesson.*
- *Read Judges 19—21. This lesson references chapter 12 in* Be Available. *It will be helpful for you to have your Bible and a copy of the commentary available as you work through this lesson.*

## Getting Started

### From the Commentary

After reading these three chapters, if you were to scan your daily newspaper or weekly news magazine, you'd have to admit that times haven't changed too much. For in these closing pages of Judges you find reports of wife abuse, blatant homosexuality, gang rape leading to murder, injustice, brother killing brother, and even kidnapping. It's the kind of narrative that almost makes you agree with British essayist Samuel Johnson, who said back in 1783, "I have lived to see things all as bad as they can be." What would he say today?

Of course, events like these are the daily food of people who enjoy TV violence, and researchers tell us that what happens on the screens is often duplicated on the streets. According to a study by the American Psychological Association, there are five violent acts per hour in prime-time TV programs, and on Saturday mornings when the children watch cartoons, violent acts per hour multiply five times (*USA Today*, August 2, 1993). When a nation is entertained by violence, is there much hope for that nation?

—*Be Available*, page 165

1. What happens to a society when evil isn't dealt with properly? How did sin in the city of Gibeah infect the tribe of Benjamin? What was the result of that sin?

2. Choose one verse or phrase from Judges 19—21 that stands out to you. This could be something you're intrigued by, something that makes you uncomfortable, something that puzzles you, something that

resonates with you, or just something you want to examine further. Write that here.

## Going Deeper

*From the Commentary*

> If you thought that the Levite Jonathan (chaps. 17—18) was a reprobate, then you'll probably conclude that the unnamed Levite in 19:1–9 was an absolute scoundrel of the basest sort. He spent most of his time partying (19:4, 6, 8, 22); he walked in darkness and jeopardized his life and the lives of those with him (vv. 9–14); he treated his concubine in the most shocking manner, while she was alive and after she was dead; and what he did to her precipitated a civil war in Israel.
>
> —*Be Available*, page 166

3. What is the lesson being taught with the story of this unnamed Levite? Why include a story about such wickedness? What does a story like this reveal about the wickedness of man apart from God? Why is that important to understand?

*More to Consider: A concubine was a lawful wife who was guaranteed only food, clothing, and marital privileges (Ex. 21:7–11; Deut. 21:10–14). Any children she bore would be considered legitimate, but because of her second-class status, they wouldn't necessarily share in the family inheritance (Gen. 25:1–6). If a man's wife was barren, he sometimes took a concubine so he could establish a family. Several notable Old Testament men had concubines, including Abraham, Jacob, Gideon, Saul, David, and Solomon. Why would the law have allowed for concubines and their children if God Himself didn't approve? What does this say about man's laws? What are some other man-made laws that go against God's desires? Ultimately, how does God's grace trump all of these laws?*

## From the Commentary

This particular concubine was unfaithful to her husband and fled to her father's house in Bethlehem for protection (Lev. 20:10). The longer she was gone, the more her husband missed her; so he traveled to Bethlehem, forgave her, and was reconciled. He and his father-in-law discovered they enjoyed each other's company and spent five days eating, drinking, and making merry. Little did the Levite realize that he really had nothing to be happy about because tragedy was stalking his marriage.

—*Be Available*, page 166

4. In what ways does this Levite illustrate the careless attitude of many believers today? How are they acting like "children of the night"? (See 1 Thess. 5:1–8.) When his nation was so far from God, how could this Levite waste his time eating, drinking, and making merry?

## From Today's World

Despite the negative aspects of the Levite's frivolous life, there is indeed "a time to laugh" (Eccl. 3:4), and God wants us to enjoy His gifts (1 Tim. 6:17). Yet in many of today's churches, the laughter of "religious entertainment" surpasses or supplants the holy hush of worship. Instead of a place for worship and study, church attempts to compete with popular movies and music and other entertainments that could draw a crowd. Many sanctuaries have become theaters, and worship services have more in common with performances than humble worship or thoughtful learning.

5. Why are churches so drawn to the idea of entertaining the people? Is there anything wrong with entertaining at church? Why or why not? Can churches be both places of worship and sources of entertainment? If so, how? And what are the dangers or risks of focusing too much on entertainment?

## From the Commentary

> During the period of the judges, it was dangerous to
> travel in the daytime (5:6) and even more so at night. The
> Levite didn't want to stay in Jerusalem because it was in
> the hands of the pagan Jebusites. Thus he pressed on four
> miles to Gibeah so he could be with his own people. *But
> the men of Gibeah turned out to be as wicked as the heathens
> around them!*
>
> To begin with, nobody in Gibeah welcomed the visitors
> and opened their home to care for them. Since the Levite
> had plenty of provisions for his party and his animals, he
> wouldn't have been a burden to anybody, but nobody took
> them in. Hospitality is one of the sacred laws of the East,
> and no stranger was to be neglected, but only one man in
> the city showed any concern, and he was an Ephraimite.
> He not only took them into his home but also used his
> own provisions to feed them and their animals.
>
> —*Be Available*, page 167

6. Why are God's people commanded to practice hospitality? What did
that mean in the time of the judges? What does that mean today? (See
1 Tim. 3:2; Titus 1:8.)

*From the Commentary*

> Gibeah had become like Sodom, a city so wicked that
> God wiped it off the face of the earth (Gen. 19). The men
> of the city were indulging in immoral practices that were
> contrary to nature (Rom. 1:24–27) and the laws of God
> (Lev. 18:22; 20:13; see 1 Cor. 6:9–10). The word "know"
> in Judges 19:22 means "to have sexual experience with."
> These sinners were excited because a new man was in
> town, and they wanted to enjoy him.
>
> —*Be Available*, page 168

7. How are the actions of the host in this story like what Lot did in Sodom?
Why would a father offer his own daughter as a sacrifice to the lusts of a
mob? What gifts from God do you possibly devalue in an effort to please
others?

*From the Commentary*

> The Levite's gruesome announcement produced the
> results that he wanted: Leaders and soldiers from the

entire nation, except Benjamin (Judg. 20:3) and Jabesh-gilead (21:8–9), came together at Mizpah to determine what to do. After hearing the Levite's indictment of the men of Gibeah, the people of Israel delivered a verdict and made a vow. The verdict was that the men of Gibeah were guilty and should be handed over to the authorities to be slain (Deut. 13:12–18). The vow was that none of the tribes represented would give their daughters in marriage to the men of Benjamin (Judg. 21:1–7).

—*Be Available*, page 169

8. What did the verdict reveal about the people of Israel? Why were they so tough on the men of Gibeah? Why did they choose to punish the tribe of Benjamin? How would this particular punishment have been detrimental to the tribe of Benjamin?

*More to Consider: The eleven tribes had agreed "as one" (Judg. 20:1) to attack Gibeah, but first they sent representatives throughout the tribe of Benjamin, calling for the people to confess their wickedness and hand over the guilty men. According to Leviticus 20:13, homosexuals were to be put to death, but that wasn't the crime the tribes were judging. What exactly were they judging? (See Deut. 13:12–18.)*

## From the Commentary

The representatives of the eleven tribes went to the tabernacle at Shiloh (Judg. 18:31; 1 Sam. 1:9) and sought the mind of the Lord, either by casting lots (Judg. 20:9) or by the priest using the Urim and Thummim (Ex. 28:30). God gave them permission to do battle, with the tribe of Judah leading the attack. That first day, God allowed the Benjamites to win and kill 22,000 Israelite soldiers.

The eleven tribes wept before the Lord and again sought His will. Note that "the children of Benjamin" in Judges 20:18 becomes "Benjamin my brother" in verse 23. Perhaps this was one reason why God permitted the Israelites to lose that first battle. It gave them an opportunity to reflect on the fact that they were fighting their own flesh and blood. But on the second day of the war, Benjamin won again, this time killing 18,000 men. The situation was very grim.

—*Be Available*, page 171

9. Why did the eleven tribes seek God's face a second time? What did they do differently this time? What was God's response? What does this reveal about God's relationship with His people during this season in history?

## From the Commentary

Once their anger cooled off, the eleven tribes realized that they had just about eliminated a tribe from the nation of Israel, and this made them weep (Judg. 21:2, 15). They offered sacrifices to the Lord, but there's no record that the people humbled themselves, confessed their sin, and sought the help of the Lord. Previously, the Lord had revealed His will to them (20:18, 23, 28), but there's no evidence that they received His word after the battle was over.

I may be wrong, but I suspect that the Lord wasn't pleased with the people of Benjamin because they still hadn't confessed their sin and admitted they were wrong. The 600 soldiers who were stranded on the rock of Rimmon still weren't seeking God's face. They were simply fleeing from the victorious army. Had somebody suggested that

they all meet the Lord at Shiloh and get the matter settled
with the Lord, it might have made a difference.

—*Be Available*, page 172

10. Review Judges 21:1–25. Instead of getting directions from the Lord, where did the eleven tribes turn to solve the problem? (See also James 3:13–18.) How did they plan on solving the problem? What was wrong with this approach?

## Looking Inward

Take a moment to reflect on all that you've explored thus far in this study of Judges 19—21. Review your notes and answers and think about how each of these things matters in your life today.

*Tips for Small Groups: To get the most out of this section, form pairs or trios and have group members take turns answering these questions. Be honest and as open as you can in this discussion, but most of all, be encouraging and supportive of others. Be sensitive to those who are going through particularly difficult times and don't press for people to speak if they're uncomfortable doing so.*

11. Do you see your church experience as more worship or entertainment? Why? What do you hope to get from your church experience? To what extent are your expectations focused on God? To what extent are they focused on you?

12. What are some ways you practice hospitality? Describe a time when someone offered you hospitality. Based on your experiences, why does God encourage His people to practice hospitality? How does doing so reveal God or grow a believer's faith?

13. Think about a time when you decided to ignore God's direction and follow your own ideas about how to solve a problem. What was the result? How would things have been different if you'd listened to God? How was God still able to use that situation for your benefit?

## Going Forward

14. Think of one or two things that you have learned that you'd like to work on in the coming week. Remember that this is all about quality, not quantity. It's better to work on one specific area of life and do it well than to work on many and do poorly (or to be so overwhelmed that you simply don't try).

Do you want to take a step to deal with evil in the world? Be specific. Go back through Judges 19—21 and put a star next to the phrase or verse that is most encouraging to you. Consider memorizing this verse.

*Real-Life Application Ideas: Determining what is right and what is wrong would seem to be a rather basic, simple thing. But sometimes the answer isn't so clear. This week, come up with a list of all the resources you might draw upon in order to make a difficult decision about right or wrong. Share that list with friends and your small-group leader, and keep adding to it until you have a comprehensive resource for those difficult decisions. Keep that list handy for the next time you need it. And in all things, ask God to direct you to the wisdom necessary to determine what is right in any given situation.*

## Seeking Help

15. Write a prayer below (or simply pray one in silence), inviting God to work on your mind and heart in those areas you've noted in the Going Forward section. Be honest about your desires and fears.

*Notes for Small Groups:*

- *Look for ways to put into practice the things you wrote in the Going Forward section. Talk with other group members about your ideas and commit to being accountable to one another.*

- *During the coming week, ask the Holy Spirit to continue to reveal truth to you from what you've read and studied.*

# Summary and Review

*Notes for Small Groups: This session is a summary and review of this book. Because of that, it is shorter than the previous lessons. If you are using this in a small-group setting, consider combining this lesson with a time of fellowship or a shared meal.*

*Before you begin …*
- *Pray for the Holy Spirit to reveal truth and wisdom as you go through this lesson.*
- *Briefly review the notes you made in the previous sessions. You will refer back to previous sections throughout this bonus lesson.*

## Looking Back

1. Over the past eight lessons, you've examined Judges. What expectations did you bring to this study? In what ways were those expectations met?

2. What is the most significant personal discovery you've made from this study?

3. What surprised you most about Judges? What, if anything, troubled you?

## Progress Report

4. Take a few moments to review the Going Forward sections of the previous lessons. How would you rate your progress for each of the things you chose to work on? What adjustments, if any, do you need to make to continue on the path toward spiritual maturity?

5. In what ways have you grown closer to Christ during this study? Take a moment to celebrate those things. Then think of areas where you feel you still need to grow and note those here. Make plans to revisit this study in a few weeks to review your growing faith.

## Things to Pray About

6. Judges is a book about listening to God and being available to His guidance rather than going your own way. As you reflect on what you've learned, ask God to make you available to Him and to make it abundantly clear what paths to take as you pursue a life of faith.

7. The messages in Judges include trust, obedience, faith, overcoming seemingly impossible odds, and letting God lead you. Spend time praying for each of these topics.

8. Whether you've been studying this in a small group or on your own, there are many other Christians working through the very same issues you discovered while examining Judges. Take time to pray for each of them, that God would reveal truth, that the Holy Spirit would guide you, and that each person might grow in spiritual maturity according to God's will.

## A Blessing of Encouragement

Studying the Bible is one of the best ways to learn how to be more like Christ. Thanks for taking this step. In closing, let this blessing precede you and follow you into the next week while you continue to marinate in God's Word:

*May God light your path to greater understanding as you review the truths found in Judges and consider how they can help you grow closer to Christ.*

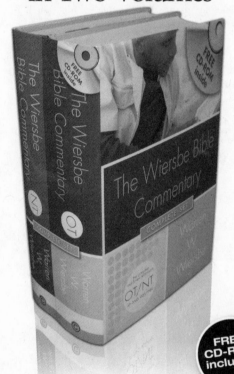

# The "BE" series . . .

For years pastors and lay leaders have embraced Warren W. Wiersbe's very accessible commentary of the Bible through the individual "BE" series. Through the work of David C. Cook Global Mission, the "BE" series is part of a library of books made available to indigenous Christian workers. These are men and women who are called by God to grow the kingdom through their work with the local church worldwide. Here are a few of their remarks as to how Dr. Wiersbe's writings have benefited their ministry.

"Most Christian books I see are priced too high for me . . .
I received a collection that included 12 Wiersbe
commentaries a few months ago and I have
read every one of them.
I use them for my personal devotions every day and they
are incredibly helpful for preparing sermons.
The contribution David C. Cook is making to the
church in India is amazing."
—Pastor E. M. Abraham, Hyderabad, India

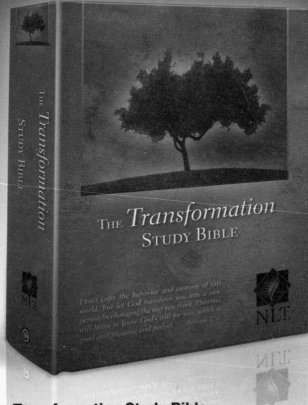